Essential Skills for
Reading College Texts

NEW ENGLAND INSTITUTE
OF TECHNOLOGY
LEARNING RESOURCES CENTER

DATE DUE

DEMCO 38-297

Books of Related Interest

Critical Thinking: Reading and Writing across the Curriculum
Anne Bradstreet Grinols, Parkland College

Opportunity for Skillful Reading, Fifth Edition
Irwin L. Joffe, formerly Phoenix College

Reading Skills for Successful Living, Third Edition
Irwin L. Joffe, formerly Phoenix College

College Reading I, Second Edition
Minnette Lenier, Los Angeles Pierce College
Janet Maker, formerly Los Angeles Pierce College

College Reading II, Third Edition
Janet Maker, formerly Los Angeles Pierce College
Minnette Lenier, Los Angeles Pierce College

College Reading III
Janet Maker, formerly Los Angeles Pierce College
Minnette Lenier, Los Angeles Pierce College

Integrating College Study Skills: Reasoning in Reading, Listening, and Writing
Peter Elias Sotiriou, Los Angeles City College

Essential Skills for Reading College Texts

Diane W. Creel

Tompkins Cortland Community College

Wadsworth Publishing Company
Belmont, California
A Division of Wadsworth, Inc.

English Editor: Angela Gantner
Production Editor: Deborah Cogan
Managing Designer: Carolyn Deacy
Print Buyer: Barbara Britton
Designer: Leigh McLellan
Copy Editor: Jennifer Gordon
Compositor: Graphic Typesetting Service, Inc.
Cover Designer: John Osborne
Signing Representative: Serina Beauparlant

Acknowledgments are listed on p. 190.

Printed in the United States of America   49

1 2 3 4 5 6 7 8 9 10———93 92 91 90 89

Library of Congress Cataloging-in-Publication Data

Creel, Diane W., 1940–
    Essential skills for reading college texts/
    Diane W. Creel.
        p.   cm.
    Includes index.
    ISBN 0-534-09888-6
    1. Reading (Higher education) 2. Study,
Method of. I. Title.
LB2395.3.C73 1989
428.4′07′11—dc19   88-22605
                                                CIP

*This book is dedicated to
my mother, LaFran Wallick,
who thought I should
and
my husband, Richard,
who thought I could.*

Contents

7　Recognizing Patterns of Organization, 139

8　Reading for Studying, 170

Preface

Let's be honest. A student who is underprepared to read college texts is in trouble. The student, the instructor, and the institution all want to get that student "up to speed" as quickly as possible. This book is intended to aid in that task by focusing on those skills essential for reading college textbooks.

As an instructor of developmental reading courses for a number of years, I found myself, like other developmental educators, facing classes of students with a wide range of abilities, motivations, interests, and purposes. My concern was always the same: how to prepare students to read college-level texts in the amount of time they were given. Over the years, I identified those reading skills I considered essential to textbook reading and developed a teaching approach that encouraged students to master new knowledge by building on prior knowledge. This book grew out of the materials I created to teach my students.

I had found that many texts intended for developmental reading courses tried to cover to varying degrees *all* reading skills, ranging from decoding to critical reading to rate improvement. I have chosen to include in this book those skills students need for a very specific task—understanding college textbooks—and to keep the book concise enough so that it can be covered thoroughly by developmental students in one semester. This leaves room for additional units on reading skills that are not covered in the book but that instructors feel are important.

The underlying theme of this book is that reading is a thinking activity and that unless one has made sense out of the word, the sentence, the paragraph, and the passage, one has not read. The student is continually reminded that reading is an activity that takes places in a context. For example, students are not asked to memorize a list of prefixes; rather they are asked to deduce the meaning of the prefix from words already known and to practice using prefixes in conjunction with context in order to make sense out of words in sentences and paragraphs. Students are also reminded that reading and writing are closely related and that they should use what they know about writing to learn more about reading. Finally, because the aim is to enable the student to read college textbooks, material similar to or taken from college texts has been provided for practice.

There are certain assumptions behind my approach in this book:

- The student is an adult deserving of respect.

- The student has the decoding skills necessary to read at approximately the sixth-grade level.

- The student tends to be a passive rather than an active reader.

- The student does not use textbook features effectively as an aid to comprehension.

- The student lacks reading/study skills or does not use such skills efficiently.

With those assumptions about the student in mind, I have incorporated the following features into the book:

- The tone is informal and conversational but adult, providing a non-threatening style that encourages the reader to interact with the text.

- The sentence structure and vocabulary are kept simple but mature. A conscious attempt is made to avoid sexist language.

- The reader is encouraged to build on what he or she already knows.

- There is a logical progression from the word to the sentence to the paragraph.

- Reading is always emphasized as a thinking process.

- Thinking skills are related to reading skills. For example, discussions of conditional statements, universal and particular statements, and logically equivalent statements are included. The language used in such discussions is nontechnical.

- Reading skills and writing skills are integrated, especially in the chapters on reading sentences and paragraphs. Students are encouraged to relate what they read in the text to what they have learned or are learning in composition classes.

- Study skills are introduced in the context of reading the college text and are interspersed throughout the text.

- Reading and study skills are always related to reading college textbooks.

- Dictionary skills appropriate for reading college textbooks are not isolated but are introduced in relation to other reading skills.

- Examples and exercises are taken from actual college textbooks or are typical of college textbooks.

- Exercises include both easy and difficult material, providing both an opportunity to succeed and a challenge.

The underprepared student has "a hard row to hoe." I sincerely hope that this book will make the task of both the student and the instructor easier.

It seems that prefaces always include what I think of as an Academy Award speech, where the author thanks everyone who "made this possible." I, it appears, am no exception because there are those whose made it possible for this book to be written, and they deserve recognition. My husband, Richard, was most supportive; he patiently read the early drafts, made good suggestions that strengthened the book, and graciously did the "grunt" work of getting the manuscript duplicated and mailed—several times. My son, Chris, yielded possession of the home computer so that I could work on it. Serina Beauparlant, my Wadsworth representative, encouraged me initially to write the book and continued thereafter to provide assistance and periodic pep talks. Steve Rutter, editor-in-chief of Wadsworth, was warm, encouraging, and competent and made me feel warm, encouraged, and competent in return. Two reviewers in particular, Peter Sotiriou of Los Angeles City College and Joe Cortina of Richland College in Dallas, Texas, provided me with reviews that were conscientious and replete with most useful suggestions. I would also like to thank the following people who reviewed the manuscript: Joan Davis, Austin Community College; Constance M. Jones, Grand Valley State College; John Penisten, University of Hawaii at Hilo; and Barbara G. Risser, Onondaga Community College.

Diane W. Creel
Ithaca, New York

1 Reading College Texts

The kind of reading demanded by college is different from the reading you did in high school or on the job or for recreation. College textbooks contain many new words or words used in a way that is different, perhaps, from the way you might use them in everyday language. Every sentence in a college text *looks* important and may *be* important. You know you can't learn everything in the book, but how do you decide what is absolutely necessary or essential?

Have you ever been reading a page in your college text and suddenly realize that you have been thinking about the trouble you've been having with your car or a letter you've been meaning to write or anything except what is on that page in your book? What has happened, of course, is that you shifted your concentration from the text to something else without realizing it. Most students have trouble concentrating on reading their texts at one time or another. It seems clear, doesn't it, that you cannot take in the information in your text if you are thinking about something else.

Here is another situation that might sound familiar to you. You have been reading *and* concentrating on the textbook. You get to the end of the section or the chapter you are reading, and you say, "Well, I read it, but I sure did not understand it." In this case you have not comprehended what you have read. You may have looked at every word on the page and you may have even understood each word. But at the end of the page you have to admit that you did not understand whatever it was that all those words added up to. It is very difficult to remember what you do not understand. The only way is to memorize it. But it also seems clear, doesn't it, that you cannot memorize the entire textbook.

Sometimes students know why they do not understand what they read. There are too many words that they can't figure out or that they don't know the meaning of. They might try at first to look up the words they don't know in the dictionary, but soon they stop because it just takes too much time. They might try to guess what the word means, but this doesn't feel like the right thing to do. You may be one of these students.

And then there is the student who sits reading in the library and looks around at the other students studying there. She notices that other students are underlining things in their texts. What is it they are underlining? Why are they doing this? Should she be underlining too? How can she decide what to underline? Are these questions you have asked yourself?

Finally there is the student who lost points on a test or a project because he didn't follow the directions. Ever done that? Probably you were told to "read the directions carefully next time." Problem is you thought you were reading the directions carefully this time.

Students experience problems like the ones just described because they lack certain essential skills necessary to read college textbooks effectively and efficiently. This book will help you learn those skills and put them into practice.

The key to reading better is to practice the necessary skills. In that way reading is like tennis. You cannot learn to play tennis well simply by reading about how to do it. You have to practice. Similarly you cannot learn to read well simply by reading about how to do it. You have to put the skills you learn in this book into practice. You will have a chance to practice the essential skills for reading college texts in this book, of course, but the best place to practice the skills is in the textbooks you are required to read in your other college classes.

The most important thing is that you decide to try to improve your reading. You already know a lot about how to read. What you want to do is to build on what you know to become a better, more efficient reader so that the time you spend reading your college texts is as effective as possible.

Reading Is an Act of Communication

In writing a book an author's responsibility is to communicate his or her message as clearly as possible. Communication is, however, a two-way street. The responsibility of the reader is to do all he or she can to receive the message of the author. The author's message has been received only when the reader comprehends (understands) the message. The reading skills essential for comprehending college textbooks will be discussed in the following chapters of this book.

Because reading is the process of receiving a written message, it is therefore an act of communication. What can you as a reader do to enhance that communication and thus improve your comprehension? We will be talking about this all through this book, but there are two things you can begin doing right away. First, you must pay attention to what is being said; you must concentrate. Second, you must become an active reader.

Removing Distractions to Concentration

Think about the following situation. You are receiving an important message over the telephone. Communication will be better if you have no distractions and can concentrate on receiving the message. If the dog is barking, the kids are screaming, the door bell is ringing, and something is burning on the stove, you will probably have trouble listening to what the person on the telephone is saying no matter how clearly they say it. The same thing is true of reading your textbook. A quiet study environment free of distractions, including music, will make it easier for you to concentrate and comprehend what you are reading.

Many students say that they cannot study without music. If you feel this way, try this experiment. For one hour as you read with music, each time you find yourself listening to the music make a mark on a piece of paper. Make a mark each time you realize that you know what song is being played, each time you find yourself singing or humming along silently or aloud. Then look at the number of marks. For each mark you recorded, you shifted your concentration from reading to the music for a period of time. You might be surprised how much of the hour you spent listening to music rather than reading. In addition, each time you returned to the reading, you first had to spend some time finding your place; then you probably had to back up and reread a little. The result is more time wasted. Finally, it is simply harder to understand and remember what you are reading if your concentration is constantly broken. Imagine how hard it would be to understand what someone was saying to you on the telephone if the message was constantly interrupted by music.

If you are used to reading with music, at first it will be difficult to read without it. Some students say that when they try to read without music, they are distracted by the silence! It might take some time to become accustomed to the lack of music. Give it at least three weeks. Old habits are sometimes hard to break.

How you handle distractions involving family members or roommates depends on the situation. Sometimes simply making the person aware that he or she is creating a distraction is enough. If the person is unwilling or unable to stop being a distraction, you may have to remove yourself and find another place to study. If your children are constantly tugging at your sleeve, remember that young children do not have a realistic sense of time. To tell them you will be with them "in a minute" or "in a little while" does not reassure them. Try setting a kitchen timer for a period of time. Tell them that when the timer goes off, you will turn your full attention to them. If you commute to classes, try to schedule study time on campus before returning home. Use the hours late at night or early in the morning when others are asleep.

Distractions can be emotional as well as physical. To concentrate on your reading you need a quiet emotional environment also. Attend to problems that command your attention before you begin to read. If the problem cannot be solved today, put it on your list of things to do tomorrow. Then forget about it for now. If you are distracted by a problem during your study time, write it down on a piece of paper. Then put the paper aside until you have finished your reading. If you find that you have trouble putting aside emotional distractions even for an hour, perhaps you should seek help. The student affairs department at your college can probably help you find counseling. Or ask a classmate or instructor where you might go to talk to someone about your personal problems.

Becoming an Active Reader by Previewing

Let's return to the situation where you are receiving an important message over the telephone. Clearly, if there are no distractions you will be able to concentrate better on the message. Let's say, however, that you were not expecting the call and had no idea what the message would be. Perhaps you were expecting a friend to call to chat with you. The phone rings, you pick it up and say hello. The person begins to communicate the message. It will probably take you a moment to realize that this is not your friend and to recognize the importance of the message. On the other hand, what if you were told to expect an important message about a particular topic at a particular time. The phone rings at the appointed hour and the message begins. Because you were expecting the call and you knew in general what the message would be about, you are ready immediately to concentrate and understand what is being said.

In a similar manner, if you have some idea about the topic of the textbook chapter and what is important about that topic before you begin to read the chapter, you are ready from the first to concentrate on what is important. To use another analogy or comparison, no intelligent person would begin an automobile trip to a place he had never been before by just getting into the car and driving in whatever direction struck his fancy. He might arrive at his destination but it would be by chance, and the probability is fairly low that he would actually arrive. Even if he did arrive, he might not realize that he was there! Or, because he was not sure where he was going and did not know what to look for, he would get lost without knowing for a very long time that he was lost. In contrast, the intelligent person would get a road map, mark his route, and note what to look for so as not to lose his way. He would go over the route in his mind and then check the map to see if he were right. As he drove to his destination, he would constantly check the map, look for the landmarks he had noted, watch for road signs.

The student who reads a textbook chapter by beginning with the first word of the first sentence in the first paragraph and plowing through to the end—or quitting in confusion, frustration, or boredom—is like the person who tries to drive to an unfamiliar destination without a road map. The intelligent student will first preview or survey the chapter just as the intelligent driver studies the road map.

To preview a chapter, first read the title of the chapter to find out what the topic will be. If there is a list of chapter objectives, read it because this is a list of the main ideas in the chapter. Then read the heading of each section of the chapter. The heading is the title of that section and perhaps will indicate the main idea of that section. Also note any illustrations, graphs, tables, or diagrams. These graphic aids are used to illustrate visually the most important points in the chapter. Next, if there is a summary at the end of the chapter, read it carefully because it will include the main ideas of the chapter. If the material in the chapter is unfamiliar to you, the summary may be hard to understand, but it will give you an idea of what to look for when you read the chapter. In addition, you may find questions at the end of the chapter. Read them. You may not be able to answer them, of course, but again they will indicate what information in the chapter is important to learn. Finally, you may find either at the beginning or the end of the chapter a list of technical terms, perhaps with definitions. Reading through the list will also help you know what to look for when you read. Previewing or surveying the chapter to prepare yourself to receive the message of the chapter is one way to participate actively in the reading process.

Becoming an Active Reader by Asking Questions

Return now once more to the important telephone message. You are expecting the call and have some idea of what the message will be. You have removed all distractions so you can concentrate on what is being said. The call comes and the message is delivered. Do you simply listen without comment and hang up? Probably not. If you did, after hanging up you might worry about whether you heard the message completely and correctly. On the contrary, because the message is so important, you ask questions to make sure you have understood. You repeat the important points of the message to get confirmation that you heard accurately. In other words, you take an active part in the communication process.

A second way to become an active reader is to hold a silent conversation with the author as you read. The active reader engages in a questioning process as he or she reads. Look at this simple paragraph.

> Unlike oranges, which are only one color, apples come in different colors. When they are ripe, apples may be red, yellow, or green although most apples are red in color. Granny Smith apples are an example of an apple that is green when ripe.

An active reader might hold a conversation with the author of this paragraph that goes something like this:

> So, what are you going to talk about in this paragraph? Looks like it will be about apples.
>
> What points are you going to make about apples? Your point seems to be that apples come in different colors.
>
> Can you prove your point that apples come in different colors? Oh, yes, you say that apples are red, yellow, and green.
>
> Green? Really? Could you give me an example of a green apple? Oh, yes, the Granny Smith apple.

Another way of engaging in a questioning process while reading is to turn the heading of the section of the chapter into a question. Then read to find the answer to your question. At the end of the section, stop and see if you can recite (say aloud in your own words) the answer to the question you formed. The active reader also uses the pattern of organization of the section or the paragraph to select what is important to learn. The most important way to improve reading comprehension is to become an active reader who asks questions while reading, and the most important question is "What is important to learn?" You will learn how to do this as you complete the chapters in this book.

Becoming an Active Reader by Marking the Textbook

A third way to become an active reader is to mark your textbook as you read. To understand how marking the text can enhance reading comprehension, consider the following situation: Let's say you receive a lengthy letter that lists in great detail a number of steps you must complete to collect $10 million you have won in a contest. If you fail to do any of the things listed in the letter, you lose the money. It is doubtful that you would just read the letter over quickly and throw it away. Rather, you would take a pen and mark the details so you would not forget anything. I cannot guarantee that you will win $10 million if you mark your textbook, but I can guarantee you will improve your reading comprehension.

Some students do not mark in their texts because it seems wrong, probably because in high school they were told *not* to mark their texts. However, unlike high school texts, these are *your* college textbooks that you have purchased. They are your property, and you certainly have the right to mark in them. Other students don't mark their texts because the books are expensive. It seems wrong to mess them up. Remember that the text is a tool you must use in order to learn in college. A student who doesn't mark the text because it is expensive is analogous to a carpenter who buys an expensive tool to use in his profession and then refuses to take it out of the package because he hates to mess it up.

Finally, some students do not mark their texts because they want to resell them and think that they will receive more for them if the books are not marked. Some college bookstores buy back texts at the end of the semester. However, there may be certain restrictions on what texts they will buy back. For example, some bookstores will not buy back a text if it will not be used in the next semester, if the text for that particular course has been changed, or if a new edition of the text has been ordered. If you plan on selling your text back to the bookstore at the end of the semester, check on any restrictions there may be. You may very carefully avoid marking your text so you can sell it back only to find that the bookstore does not intend to buy back that particular text. Even if the bookstore will buy back your text, many do not pay any more for an unmarked book. You will receive the same amount of money for a marked text as for an unmarked text. But most importantly, consider what you are doing to yourself by not marking your text. You are denying yourself a method for improving your reading comprehension. Do you really want to do that to yourself? In the following chapters you will learn how to mark your textbook in an effective manner.

Summary

The kind of reading necessary to understand college texts is different from other types of reading. College textbooks contain many words that may be unfamiliar. The chapter may be packed with information—all of which looks very important and may, in fact, be important. The reader of a college textbook needs to be able to decide what is important to learn.

Reading is an act of communication because the reader must receive the written message of the author. The author's message is not received unless it is understood. Because reading is an act of communication, the reader should do everything possible to improve that communication. First, the reader must concentrate. Removing distractions will enhance concentration. Second, the reader must take an active part in the process of reading. Previewing or surveying the chapter before reading it, asking questions while reading the chapter, and learning to mark the text in an effective manner are three ways to become an active reader.

Surveying, asking questions, and marking the text take more time than just passively reading the chapter beginning with the first word, first sentence, first paragraph. However, it is time well spent because the payoff is better concentration and more complete comprehension. Passive reading does not guarantee that you will understand and remember what you have read. If you have ever said, "I read it, but I don't understand it" or "I read it, but I can't remember it," you are probably a passive reader. Becoming an active reader will help you fulfill your responsibility in the reading/communication process.

Use the following exercises to test yourself so that you can identify your reading strengths and weaknesses.

EXERCISE 1

Read the following sentences and then match the words listed below them with the meaning of the words as they are used in the sentences.

1. You know you can't learn everything in the book, but how do you decide what is absolutely necessary or essential?

2. The author's message has been received only when the reader comprehends (understands) the message.

3. Because reading is the process of receiving a written message, it is therefore an act of communication.

4. What can you as a reader do to enhance that communication and thus improve your comprehension?

5. Some students say that when they try to read without music, they are distracted by the silence!

6. It might take some time to become accustomed to the lack of music.

7. Attend to problems that command your attention before you begin to read.

8. To use another analogy or comparison, no intelligent person would begin an automobile trip to a place he had never been before by just getting into the car and driving in whatever direction struck his fancy.

9. The intelligent student will first preview or survey the chapter just as the intelligent driver studies the road map.

10. At the end of the section, stop and see if you can recite (say aloud in your own words) the answer to the question you formed.

	Word	**Meaning**
_____ 1.	essential	a. say aloud in your own words
_____ 2.	comprehend	b. used to
_____ 3.	reading	c. process of receiving a written message
_____ 4.	enhance	d. comparison
_____ 5.	distracted	e. necessary
_____ 6.	accustomed	f. understand
_____ 7.	attend	g. preview
_____ 8.	analogy	h. pulled or drawn away
_____ 9.	survey	i. take care of
_____ 10.	recite	j. increase, strengthen

EXERCISE 2

Fill in the blank with the correct word.

1. The key to reading better is to _____ the necessary skills.

2. Reading is an act of _____.

3. The author's message has not been received if the reader does not

_____ the message.

4. Distractions interfere with _____ and make it hard to comprehend what you are reading.

5. Reading comprehension is improved by being an _____

reader who surveys, asks questions, and marks the text.

EXERCISE 3

Mark the following sentences with T for true or F for false. (The statements should be marked true if they are made by the author in this chapter, whether or not you agree with the statements.) You may want to discuss with your instructor those statements with which you disagree.

_____ 1. Reading in college is different from the reading done in high school or on the job.

_____ 2. You must memorize everything in your college textbooks.

_____ 3. Distractions can be emotional.

_____ 4. Listening to music when you read does not interfere with concentration.

_____ 5. The most efficient way to read a textbook chapter is to begin with the first word in the chapter and read to the end without stopping.

_____ 6. Surveying is a way of preparing yourself to look for the most important points in a chapter when you read it.

_____ 7. An active reader asks questions while reading.

_____ 8. You should not mark in your textbooks.

_____ 9. You should read the summary of a chapter only after you have finished reading the entire chapter.

_____ 10. Reading actively takes more time but results in better understanding than does reading passively.

2 Context Clues

A major requirement you will quickly note in your college classes is the large amount of reading you are expected to do on your own outside of class. In this reading, you will run across words that you do not know. Many beginning college students try to be as conscientious as possible and look up in the dictionary each word that they are unsure of or do not know. This practice usually does not last too long because it takes a lot of time. Besides, a word may have many definitions, and the student might not be sure which meaning is best in that case.

Soon the student will begin to skip over words that are unfamiliar. Sometimes this practices does not interfere with comprehension (understanding). However, each time you skip over a word, it is like leaving a blank or a hole on the page. If you skip too many words, you end up with a page of reading that is full of blanks. No wonder, then, that you get to the bottom of the page without understanding what it is you have read.

So, what is the solution? When you come to a word that you are unsure of or are unfamiliar with, most of you don't just skip it. Most of you will think about what the sentence is saying and make a guess about what the unfamiliar word might mean. Good for you! When you use the sentence to figure out what the word means, you are using context. The word *context* means "the setting of a word." We are concerned in this book with reading skills essential (necessary) for textbook reading. The setting of a word in a text is the sentence it is in. Consider the word *nuts* in the following sentence that might be found in a text used in a food preparation course.

The drinks before dinner should be served with **nuts** and other snacks.

Now look at the following sentence that might be found in a mechanical technology text.

> Choosing the correct **nuts** for the type of bolts used and the particular job to be done is very important.

The context of the word *nuts* is different, and the meaning of the word *nuts* is also different. In the first sentence the word *nuts* means the edible kernel of a fruit or seed with a hard shell. In the second sentence, the word *nuts* means a block of metal with a threaded hole designed to hold a bolt or screw. You can eat the first nut but not the second!

You have just become aware of an important concept: The context of a word determines the meaning of the word. The meaning of a word depends on the meaning of the sentence it is in. So you can use what you know about what a sentence is saying to figure out what a particular word in that sentence means.

Another important concept to remember about using context to discover the meaning of a word is that in a textbook you will not be dealing with words in isolation; the word will be in a sentence, and the sentence will be in a paragraph. If the sentence (the context of the word) is not enough to decide on the meaning of an unfamiliar word, it may be that the paragraph the sentence is in (the context of the sentence) will give you enough information to make a decision.

Also remember that using context clues is only one method of figuring out the meanings of unknown words. Using context to decide on a word's meaning is guessing about the word's meaning. Guessing is not an exact science. Some of your guesses will be good, but others may not be. In addition, not every sentence will contain context clues that will help you determine a word's meaning. But, not to worry. There are other ways to figure out the meanings of words, and we will talk about them in the next chapter.

One final note of caution. When you use context to decide on a word's meaning, you are guessing what the word *might* mean. The trick is to make your guess a good one. A good guess is one that is deduced (drawn or derived) from evidence or information. The kind of guess we mean here is what can be called an "educated guess." An educated guess is not a wild, haphazard one but rather is one that is based on evidence or information. When we use context to deduce a word's meaning, we become like detectives looking for evidence or clues to solve a mystery. Fortunately for us, writers often give clues to a word's meaning. Once you know what those clues are and how to use them, you can become more efficient in figuring out what words mean from the context.

Context Clues: Direct Definition

Sometimes an author will simply tell you what a word means, and if he or she takes the trouble to give you the word's definition, it must be because the word is a very important one. Usually words that are defined by the author are part of the **technical** or **specialized** vocabulary of the course. Such words may be words used in one way in everyday language and in a more specialized, restricted way in a particular field of study. For example, when you see the word *right*, the definition that comes immediately to mind is probably "correct" or perhaps a direction as in "turn to the right." However, if the author is describing *right angles*, he or she is not describing angles that are correct or angles that point in a particular direction: The author is describing angles of 90 degrees.

> A **right angle** is an angle of 90 degrees formed by two lines perpendicular to each other.

Sometimes the word will be one that is special to a particular field of study and is not used in everyday language. These words may not even be in your dictionary. *Googol* is such a word.

> A **googol** is defined as the numeral 1 followed by 100 zeroes.

Words that are a part of the specialized or technical vocabulary of a course must be understood and learned. You should begin marking these words and their definitions in your textbooks. One way to do this is to put a box around the word and underline the definition.

> A **microcomputer** refers to a desk-top computer system with limited storage.

In the sentence below, draw a box around the technical word and underline the definition.

> In sociological research, a **sample** means a group of persons selected from the larger population.

You should have drawn a box around the word *sample* and underlined the words "a group of persons selected from the larger population."

Notice in the examples above that words such as *is defined*, *refers to*, and *means* are used to signal that a definition is to follow. Notice, too, that the words defined are in boldface print. You will find that in your textbooks technical words are often in italics, boldface, or colored ink.

Remember that when you decide on the definition of a word, you are deciding what the word *means*. You might think about this concept using the following formula:

the word *means* its definition

If we use *X* for "the word" and *Y* for "its definition," we have the even shorter formula:

X means *Y*

Once you have decided on the definition, try putting it into the formula of "*X* means *Y*" and see if it makes sense.

Let's take an example that will be obvious to you.

A capital asset on the federal income tax form is defined as property you own and use for personal purposes, pleasure, or investment.

If you are not thinking as you read, you might decide that *federal income tax form* is the term being defined and "property you own and use for personal purposes, pleasure, or investment" is the definition. Using our formula of "*X* means *Y*," we would have the following:

federal income tax form *means* property you own and use for personal purposes, pleasure, or investment.

That clearly makes no sense. Reading is a thinking activity, and if your decision about what a word means makes no sense, you need to rethink your decision. What is being defined here, of course, is *capital asset*. Let's try that in our formula:

Capital asset *means* property you own and use for personal purposes, pleasure, or investment.

Now that makes sense. The words "on the federal income tax form" tell us *where* capital asset is defined as property you own and use for personal purposes, pleasure, or investment.

EXERCISE 1

In the following sentences taken from a business textbook,[1] draw a box around the technical or specialized word and underline the definition. Check your decision by using the "*X* means *Y*" formula.

1. A **trademark** is a brand that has been given legal protection.

2. A **cooperative** is an organization whose owners band together to collectively operate all or part of their industries.

3. According to the Bureau of Labor Statistics (BLS), **high-technology firms** are those companies whose research and development expenditures and number of technical employees are twice as great as the average for all manufacturing firms.

4. **Capital** is defined as the funds necessary to finance the operation of a business.

5. Accountants and business people define **profit** as the difference between revenues and expenses.

6. **Stockholders** are those people who acquire the shares of the corporation.

7. The interest rate the Federal Reserve System charges on loans to member banks is called the **discount rate.**

Context Clues: Punctuation

The context of a word is the sentence in which the word appears. Punctuation marks are a part of the sentence and can sometimes be used as context clues to help you deduce the meaning of a word. For example, writers may set off the meaning of a word by using punctuation.

> **Essential hypertension** [high blood pressure] must be carefully monitored.

The term *essential hypertension* is defined by the words "high blood pressure," which are placed in the brackets.

> She was interested in studying **psychokinesis**—the ability to move an object without touching it.

Psychokinesis is defined by the words that follow the dash, "the ability to move an object without touching it."
Sometimes the word being defined, rather than the definition, will be set off by punctuation. In that case, the definition will come right before the term.

> The most common phobia for which people seek help is the fear of open spaces (**agoraphobia**).

Agoraphobia is set off by parentheses and is defined by the words that come right before it: "the fear of open spaces."

Other punctuation that might mark off a definition are commas.

Nest building in birds is an example of an **instinct,** a pattern of behavior that doesn't have to be learned.

However, the comma may set off the word being defined rather than the definition. In that case the definition will come right before the word.

About 2 to 4 percent of the American population suffers from feelings of apprehension, or **anxiety.**

Anxiety is defined by the words that come right before it in the sentence: "feelings of apprehension." Notice that in this example the word *or* also serves to signal that a word has been defined.

The colon (:) might also set off a definition as in the following example.

Another layer of the earth's crust is formed of **metamorphic rocks:** rocks that have been changed, usually by high temperature and pressure within the crust.

Punctuation marks are important aids to comprehension. We will talk more about this later, but for now be aware of the following punctuation marks that often are used to set off the definitions of words.

Name of Punctuation Mark	Looks Like This
comma	,
dash	—
colon	:
parentheses	( )
brackets	[ ]

EXERCISE 2

In the sentences below, the technical term is in boldface print and its definition is set off by punctuation. Draw a box around the term and underline the definition.

1. The course outline, or **syllabus,** gives important information about the requirements of the course.

2. The student should be familiar with the **curriculum**—set of courses—of his or her certificate or degree program.

3. Some courses have **prerequisites:** requirements that must be met before the course can be taken.

4. A student may plan to transfer after two years at a community college to an institution that offers a **baccalaureate** [bachelor or four-year] degree program.

5. As soon as possible the student should seek to be **matriculated** (formally accepted by the college into a degree or certificate program).

EXERCISE 3

Draw a box around the technical term and underline the definition in these sentences taken from a psychology textbook.[2]

1. Allen, the fanatically fastidious college student, is plagued by **obsessions** (persistent ideas, thoughts, images, or impulses that seem senseless even to him and yet invade his consciousness against his will) and by **compulsions** (repetitive, irrational behaviors that he feels obligated to carry out even though he can't see any point to them himself).

2. Two other kinds of eating disorders, which seem to have become more common in recent years, especially among young women, are **anorexia nervosa,** a form of self-starvation that can actually lead to death, and **bulimia,** in which an individual regularly eats vast quantities of food and then purges the body of them either by induced vomiting or laxative use.

3. **Aggression**—any behavior intended to hurt someone or something—is all around us. In most places around the world, not least in the United States, this aggression often explodes into **violence,** destructive action against people or property.

4. Developmental psychologists study **physical development** (changes in the body such as height, weight, brain development, and the acquisition and refinement of motor skills); **cognitive development** (changes in thought

processes, which affect learning, language abilities, and memory); and **psychosocial development** (changes in the emotional and social aspects of personality).

EXERCISE 4

In the following passage you will find words defined directly and words defined by punctuation context clues. Draw a box around each word that is defined and underline its definition. The passage describes the structure of the human eye and is taken from a psychology textbook.[3]

Light passes first through the **cornea,** the transparent tissue in front of the eye. The cornea is made of the same material as the **sclera,** the white outer part of the eyeball, but is transparent because of the way the corneal molecules are arranged. The sclera, the "skin of the eye," contains receptors for pressure, temperature, and pain.

The light then enters the **anterior** (front) chamber of the eye. This chamber is filled with a watery fluid called **aqueous humor,** which helps to "feed" the cornea and which is continually secreted, released, and replaced.

After passing through the anterior chamber, light enters the chamber just behind it through a small hole called the **pupil.** The pupil **dilates** (opens wide) to let more light in under conditions of darkness, and it **constricts** (becomes smaller) in bright light. The size of the pupil is controlled by the **iris,** the colored part of the eye.

Separating Definition from Examples

If a child were to ask you what an elephant is and if just at that moment an elephant happened to be walking by, you would probably point to the animal and say, "There! That is an elephant." However, you haven't really told the child what an elephant is. You have simply pointed out one particular instance, or an example of an elephant.

On the other hand, if an elephant did *not* happen to walk by just as the child asked you what an elephant is, you would probably start by listing the outstanding features or characteristics of an elephant. You might say, "Well, it is a large gray animal with a trunk and large ears."

The point here is to notice that an example does not tell you the meaning of a word. It only points out one particular instance or illustration. If I were to ask you what the word *fruit* means and you were to tell me that an apple is a fruit, I still would not be sure what *fruit* means. If I used the "*X* means *Y*" formula, I would get "*fruit* means apple." However, if you told me that *fruit* means "the usually edible product of a plant, especially one having a sweet pulp and seeds," and then added "like an apple," you would have given me both the characteristics of *fruit* and an example of a fruit.

Many definitions in your textbooks will take the following form:

1. term   2. characteristic   3. example

Study the following example.

A carnivore is a meat-eating animal like the tiger.

1. The term is *carnivore*.

2. The characteristic of a carnivore is that it is a meat-eating animal.

3. The example of a carnivore is the tiger.

What is essential to learn about a term is not the example but the characteristics of the term. Examples can help us understand and remember what a term means. But an example does not tell the meaning of the term; the characteristics of a term tell its meaning.

The definitions in your texts will not always take the form of first the term, then the characteristic, and finally the example. Look at the following definition.

A herbivore such as the horse is a plant-eating animal.

term   = herbivore

characteristic = plant-eating animal

example   = horse

What is essential to learn about a herbivore is that it is a plant-eating animal, the characteristic of a herbivore. Notice that the words *such as* signal the example. Other words that signal an example are the following:

like   for instance   for example   as illustrated by

An error that many students make in their textbook reading is to mistake an example for a definition. Remember that the example gives an illustration whereas the characteristic gives the definition or meaning. Look at the following sentence that defines *ethnic group* and provides an example of that term.

> French Canadians may be defined as an ethnic group, a category of people who think of themselves and are thought of by others as possessing such shared cultural traits as religion, food preferences, and language.

Ethnic group does not *mean* French Canadians. It *means* "a category of people who think of themselves and are thought of by others as sharing cultural traits." That is the characteristic of *ethnic group*. French Canadians is, of course, an *example* of an ethnic group.

In your textbooks you should begin drawing a box around the term in a definition and underlining the characteristics of the term. Because examples are provided to help you understand the meaning of important terms, you should get into the habit of noting examples in your textbooks by drawing two lines under them. Study the following example:

An ┃omnivore┃ is an animal such as the <u>bear</u> that <u>eats both plants and meat</u>.

EXERCISE 5

In the following sentences, draw a box around the term being defined, draw one line under the definition, and draw two lines under any examples. Check your decision about the definition by using the "*X* means *Y*" formula.

1. Income can be defined as the money a person receives such as a salary or investment from stocks and bonds.

2. The value of a person's possessions, like a house and car, is referred to as wealth.

3. Wealth that produces more wealth in the form of income for the owner, as illustrated by rental property, is defined as influential wealth.

4. According to Abraham Maslow, physiological needs are those that sustain life, for example, food, clothing, and shelter.

5. Sociologists define the term institution as a widely accepted, stable group, such as the family, that develops to satisfy the basic needs of a society.

EXERCISE 6

In the following passage from a business textbook,[4] draw a box around the term being defined. Then draw a line under the definition. You should mark technical terms in your texts in this same manner.

> **Frictional unemployment** refers to the 2 to 3 percent of the labor force who are temporarily not working, but are searching for jobs. The frictionally unemployed include students leaving school and looking for jobs and other persons who are in the process of leaving old jobs and finding new ones, frequently in different cities. **Seasonal unemployment** refers to those who are currently unemployed because of the seasonal nature of their industry. Seasonal unemployment typically affects such persons as construction workers, farm workers engaged in harvesting crops, and some retail clerical workers who are employed during holiday periods. **Cyclical unemployment** involves people who are out of work because of reduced economic activity. Much of the unemployment statistics during the recession of the early 1980s resulted from workers who were laid off as a result of the stagnant economy. The fourth category, **structural unemployment,** applies to people who lack the necessary skills for employment, or those whose skills are no longer demanded.

EXERCISE 7

Many passages in textbooks are similar to the one you just read with many technical terms defined in one paragraph. It would be easier to learn the meanings of the terms in such a paragraph if you extract (take out) the term, the definition, and at least one example so you can concentrate on them. A chart is one good way to organize the essential information you need to learn from a paragraph that defines several terms. Use the paragraph in Exercise 6 to complete the following chart.

Term	Characteristic	Example
Frictional unemployment	Temporarily not working but searching for jobs	
Seasonal unemployment		
Cyclical unemployment		Workers laid off during recession in 1980s
Structural unemployment		

Context Clues: General Sense of the Sentence

So far we've been talking about using context clues to determine the meaning of technical or specialized terms. Because these words are so important to understand, authors will usually make their meaning very clear as we can see in the following examples from an economics text.[5] They may give you a direct definition:

Money is anything that is generally accepted as a means of payment for goods, services, and debt.

Or perhaps they will set off the definition with punctuation:

Recycling—the transformation of wastes into raw materials that are again usable—requires variable lengths of time, depending on what it is that is being recycled.

Or they may give you a definition plus examples:

Production or consumption of a product can yield **social spillover costs,** too. These are costs imposed on people not involved in the production or consumption of the good. If one of my neighbors opens a beauty shop at home, there will be a noticeable increase in traffic on our street. It will be necessary to supervise the kids more closely to keep them from being run over. This nuisance is a social spillover cost.

You may run into words other than specialized and technical vocabulary terms whose meanings you are unsure of. Often you can guess at the meanings of these words just from the general sense of the sentence. To prove this point, look at the following example of a sentence that has a nonsense word in it and notice that you can probably figure out from your own experience and the sense of the sentence (the context) what the nonsense word would have to mean.

He slurred his speech, stumbled when he walked, and smelled of liquor, so I guessed he was zylonk.

From the clues of slurred speech, unsteady walk, and suspicious-smelling breath, it is fairly easy to figure out that *zylonk* must mean "drunk" or "inebriated." Notice that we can replace *zylonk* with *drunk* and the sentence makes sense. Try another sentence with a nonsense word.

She was very fortunate that she was able to blachet the flames before they spread to the rest of the house.

Do you agree that *blachet* must mean to "put out" or "extinguish"?

EXERCISE 8

In the following sentences you will find some nonsense words. Think about what the sentence is saying and decide what the nonsense word would have to mean in order to make sense in the sentence. Your definition does not have to be a single word; it might be several words or a phrase. Your definition might not be exactly the same as a classmate's. Remember that when you use the context of the sentence to decide on the definition of a word, you are making an educated guess about what the word means. To test the correctness of your guess, try replacing the nonsense word with your definition. Does the sentence make sense? If it doesn't, your guess is either not correct or is not close enough.

Beneath each sentence, write a definition for the nonsense word in boldface print.

1. It is **niblock** that your registration forms be complete; otherwise you will not get credit for the class.

   Definition: _____

2. I really **proster** snakes; I don't even like to see a picture of one.

Definition: _____

3. To save money for college I had to **menate** the number of movies I go to each month.

Definition: _____

4. I was going to serve steak at my dinner party, but the price made me **cride** my plans.

Definition: _____

5. Marsha absolutely will not take another math course. Don't try to change her mind because she is **frind.**

Definition: _____

EXERCISE 9

The sentences in this exercise do not contain nonsense words. You may already know some of the boldfaced words. What is important here is not just coming up with a definition: The important thing is to *become aware* of the context clues in the sentence. So in this exercise you are asked not only to write a definition of the word but also to list the words in the sentence that serve as context clues. Do not look up any of these words in a dictionary. The first one is done for you.

1. Extroverted persons, who enjoy parties and meeting new people, are less likely to be victims of depression.

Definition: outgoing, friendly

Clue: enjoy parties and meeting new people

2. There are some things in the world that seem **inexplicable** and just have to be accepted without knowing why they happened.

Definition: _____

Clue: _____

3. He must file for bankruptcy because his business failed and he has become **insolvent** and unable to pay his bills.

Definition: _____

Clue: _____

4. He never has anything good to say about his wife and is always making **disparaging** remarks about her.

Definition: _____

Clue: _____

5. Many people are uncomfortable with change and resist any **innovation.**

Definition: _____

Clue: _____

EXERCISE 10

These sentences are somewhat more difficult. Don't succumb to temptation and look up the words in a dictionary. What is important here is that you try to make sense of the word from what the sentence seems to be saying. Sometimes you can come close enough to the word's meaning without being able to say exactly what the word means.

1. Because you are responsible for all work done in class even if you are not there, it **behooves** you to find out from your classmates or instructor what material was covered when you were absent.

Definition: _____

2. Depression often causes a person to be indifferent to his personal appearance, to lose interest in his friends and surroundings, in fact to be completely **apathetic.**

Definition: _____

3. When faced with the facts, Henry **conceded** that his position was incorrect.

Definition: _____

4. The peace talks resulted in a **diminution** of the war although the battles did not cease altogether.

Definition: _____

5. One year after winning the state lottery, Sam was bankrupt because of his **profligate** lifestyle.

   Definition: _____

6. The large size and weight of the old computers made them awkward to handle and **cumbersome** to move.

   Definition: _____

7. Anne had a tendency to be wordy, and her composition instructor was constantly asking her to reduce the **verbiage** in her papers.

   Definition: _____

8. The conditions of employment are specified in the contract, and if you are not able to agree to the requirements as **stipulated,** do not bother to apply.

   Definition: _____

9. Maria was so weakened by the **debilitating** illness that she needed months to rest and restore her strength.

   Definition: _____

10. The student was accused of **plagiarism** because he had used the words and ideas of an author without crediting the source in a footnote.

   Definition: _____

Context Clues: Contrast

Sometimes an author will give clues to a word's meaning by using contrast. For example:

   Mary was guilty, **unlike** John who was innocent.

The signal word *unlike* lets you know that two different things are going on in the sentence. In this sentence, the two different things are "Mary was guilty" and "John was innocent." If you were unsure of the word *innocent*, you could deduce that it might mean "the opposite of guilty" or "not guilty."
   Other contrast signal words are the following:

whereas	but	while
although	however	not

| even though | instead | rather than |
| on the contrary | on the other hand | nevertheless |

Try another example:

While I love spinach, my husband loathes it.

While is the contrast signal word. It lets you know that my husband and I feel differently about spinach. If I love it and he feels differently about it, then he might feel the opposite of love. So *loathe* may mean "the opposite of love," or "hate."

Notice that in this example you cannot know that my husband feels *exactly* the opposite from the way I feel about spinach. Maybe he doesn't hate it but is just indifferent. That is, he can take it or leave it. Remember that using context to deduce a word's meaning is making an educated guess from the information in the sentence. In this case, the sentence doesn't give you enough information to know that my husband feels exactly the opposite of the way I do. We can just know that he feels differently. However, in your texts you will not have just one sentence from which to make your deduction about an unfamiliar word. The sentence will be in the larger context of a paragraph that will give you more information. The more information you can gather about a word, the better your deduction will be. Our purpose here is to become more aware of how recognizing a contrast in a sentence can be a clue to a word's meaning so you can make sense of the sentence. If it is important for you to know exactly what the word means, you can look it up in the dictionary.

Now, the easiest way to come up with a word that is opposite in meaning to another is just to put *not* in front of it. The opposite of *love* is *not love*. With that in mind, try coming up with the definition of the underlined word in the following example.

Although Marsha is <u>fastidious</u>, her twin Marilyn is very sloppy.

Marsha and Marilyn are contrasted by the word *although*. If Marilyn is sloppy and Marsha is the opposite, then Marsha must be not sloppy. In the simplest terms, *fastidious* means "not sloppy."

Often an unfamiliar word will be in one sentence and the contrasting definition will be in a sentence before or after it. Look at this example:

You should review your lecture notes immediately after class to correct any errors or fill in missing information. Many students, **however,** <u>procrastinate</u> and, as a result, their notes are not as useful.

In this example, the contrast signal word is *however*. The contrast is between what you should do and what many students in fact do. You should do something to your notes *immediately*, but many students *procrastinate*. So the definition of *procrastinate* is "not immediately."

Notice that our definitions so far have been rather simple. For example, *procrastinate* is more appropriately defined as "delay or postpone." Again remember what we are trying to do here. We are trying to become *more aware* of the way context clues work. Determining the meaning of an unfamiliar word when contrast is used to define it is best done along with the general sense of the sentence.

> The picnic was a <u>fiasco</u>. **Even though** James tried to plan for every emergency, his plans for a <u>successful party</u> were spoiled by the cold rainy weather.

The contrast phrase here is *even though.* What is being contrasted is what James planned for (a successful party) and what he got (a fiasco). So *fiasco* must mean something like "the opposite of successful" or "not successful" or "failure."

There will not always be a contrast signal word or phrase. However, the sense of the sentence or sentences will tell you that the unknown word is being contrasted to a known word or phrase. Always remember that reading is a thinking process. You must *think as you read* and always try to make sense of what you are reading. Think about what the sentence is saying and what it would make sense for the unknown word to mean in the context of the sentence.

> David was unable to organize his research notes in a logical, orderly manner. As a result, his paper was **incoherent.**

Can you tell from these sentences that *incoherent* must mean "the opposite of logical and orderly"? *Incoherent* means "not logical and orderly."

It is important to remember that using context clues to determine the meaning of unfamiliar words is guessing. Guessing is not an exact science. What you are trying to do is to make those guesses as intelligent as possible.

EXERCISE 11

In the following sentences, look first for a contrast signal word or phrase. If you find one, draw a box around it. Then search for a word or phrase that might be the opposite in meaning to the word in bold print and underline it. After the sentence, write the definition of the word in bold print. Remember the definition will be the opposite of the word or phrase you underlined. The first one is done for you.

1. [Unlike] my **taciturn** brother, I <u>talk a lot</u>.

    Definition: not talk a lot

2. There was disagreement instead of **consensus** about the committee's report.

Definition: _____

3. We decided to **persevere** rather than give up.

Definition: _____

4. Jennifer had hoped the divorce would be friendly; however, her husband was very **antagonistic.**

Definition: _____

5. The instructor said she would not repeat the instructions; nevertheless, she did **reiterate** them when it became clear that most of the students were confused about what to do.

Definition: _____

EXERCISE 12

The following sentences are more difficult. Box any contrast words and write beneath the sentence the definition of the word in bold print.

1. Some courses are required whereas others are **electives.**

Definition: _____

2. English 201 cannot be taken **concurrently** in the semester with English 101 but rather must be taken after you have passed English 101.

Definition: _____

3. Some instructors do not feel strongly about class attendance; on the other hand, others are **adamant** that you must attend all classes.

Definition: _____

4. You must **substantiate** your conclusions in your research paper. Students who do not support their statements with facts will find their papers unacceptable.

Definition: _____

5. Some students expect all instructors to have the same grading system. They will find, however, a **variability** of systems.

   Definition: _____

6. A valid research project demands that if the experiment is duplicated, the results will be the same. A **disparity** of results throws doubt on the entire project.

   Definition: _____

7. Even though Evan thought he could change Marie's position on capital punishment, she remained **implacable.**

   Definition: _____

8. Rather than take data processing for credit, Stacy decided to **audit** it to see if she was interested in the subject.

   Definition: _____

9. I thought registering for courses would be easy. I found the process, on the contrary, to be **arduous.**

   Definition: _____

10. Although I sat near the front of the room so I could hear the instructor, she spoke so softly I found the lecture **inaudible.**

    Definition: _____

Putting Context Clues to Work

To become a better reader, you must practice the reading skills you have learned. The best place to practice is in the textbooks that you are reading for your other courses. Remember that context determines the meaning of the word and that the context of a word is the sentence that it is in. If you can't determine the meaning of the word from the sentence, think about the context of the sentence—the paragraph the sentence is in. Always keep in mind that reading is a thinking activity. You must think about what the context of the word (the sentence) means as well as what the context of the sentence (the paragraph) means.

Words that are defined for you by the author are usually technical or specialized words and are very important to understand. That is the reason that the author defines them for you. You must learn what the words mean in order to understand the textbook and do well in the course. Get into the habit of boxing the technical words in your texts and underlining their definitions.

It is a good idea to keep a list of the technical words you find in your texts not only because they are so important to understanding the text but also because they are often on the tests you will have in the course. You need to organize the words you want to learn so that you can study them. Some students like to make a chart with the term, its characteristics, and an example as we did in Exercise 7.

Other students like to make a note card for each word that they need to learn. They put the word and the page number from the text where they found the word on one side of the card and the definition and an example on the other side of the card. Then they practice by looking at the word and trying to say the definition. Of course, they check to see if they are correct by flipping the card over and looking at the definition. You could mark a plus (+) each time you say the definition correctly. If you get three pluses, you probably know the word and can put the card aside. Each time you fail to get the definition, give yourself a minus (−). If you get three minuses, that means you don't understand what the word means. Those words you are having trouble with are the ones you should concentrate on.

If you cannot say the definition correctly after three tries, go back to the page where you first found the word and read about it again. In other words, put the word back into context and see if the context will help you understand the word. Check to see if there is a glossary at the end of your textbook. A glossary is a dictionary for that book and will define the words as they are used in the book. You can try looking up the word in a regular dictionary. You might find several meanings for the word, and you will have to use the context of the word (the sentence in your textbook where you found the word) to help decide which of the meanings is the one you should select for the word as it is used in your textbook. Try the "*X* means *Y*" formula to help you decide if the definition you selected makes sense in the context of your textbook. If you still have trouble, ask the instructor or a classmate to explain the word to you.

You should organize the words you need to learn and start studying them as soon as you finish reading the chapter. Many students just read the chapter when it is assigned and wait until immediately before the test to start studying. What a mistake! What they discover, of course, is that there is too much to study, and they panic. If you organize the words into a chart or make cards, you can start studying right now. Then when a test is announced, you will find that you already know much of the material. You will feel more confident and will not be as nervous about the test.

The following exercises are taken from college textbooks and will allow you to try using context clues. The best place to practice, however, is in the textbooks you are reading for other courses.

EXERCISE 13

In the following passage, taken from a book on microcomputers,[6] draw a box around technical words and then complete the chart following the passage.

The **microprocessor** is the place in the computer where all of the actual processing takes place. This processing is done in basically four steps called the **process cycle:**

1. The instruction the computer is to carry out is **fetched** from memory and brought into the processor.
2. The instruction is then **decoded,** or translated, so the computer will know what to do.
3. The computer will actually **execute,** or carry out, the instruction.
4. The results of the execution are **stored** back into the memory.

Term	Definition
microprocessor	_____
process cycle	_____
fetched	_____
decoded	_____
execute	_____
stored	_____

EXERCISE 14

Draw a box around the technical words and draw a line under their definitions in the following passage taken from an introductory biology book.[7] Then complete the chart that follows the passage.

All matter, including the most complex living organisms, is made up of combinations of *elements*, which are substances that cannot be broken down by ordinary chemical means. The smallest particle of an element is an *atom*. There are 92 naturally occurring elements, each differing from the others in the structure of its atoms.

The atoms of each different element have a characteristic number of positively charged particles, called *protons*, in their nuclei. [Nuclei is the plural form of nucleus, which is the central portion of the atom.] For example, an atom of hydrogen, the lightest of the elements, has 1 proton in its nucleus; an atom of the heaviest naturally occurring element, uranium, has 92 protons in its nucleus. The number of protons in the nucleus of a particular atom is called its *atomic number*.

Outside the nucleus of an atom are negatively charged particles, the *electrons*, which are attracted by the positive charge of the protons. The number of electrons in an atom equals the number of protons in its nucleus. The electrons determine the chemical properties of atoms, and chemical reactions involve changes in the numbers and energy of these electrons.

Atoms also contain *neutrons*, which are uncharged particles of about the same weight as protons. These, too, are found in the nucleus of the atom, where they seem to have a stabilizing effect.

Term	Definition
elements	_____
atom	_____

protons   _____

atomic number   _____

electrons   _____

neutrons   _____

EXERCISE 15

From a textbook you are reading for another course, find ten sentences in which a word is defined directly or by punctuation context clues. The words can be technical or specialized words, but they do not have to be.

Write out each sentence as you found it in your book. At the end of the sentence put the number of the page where you found the sentence. Sometimes you will find the word in one sentence and the definition in the sentence that comes right after it. In that case write out both sentences.

Draw a box around the word being defined and draw a line under the definition. Draw two lines under examples if the sentence includes them.

EXERCISE 16

Using the sentences in Exercise 15, make a card for each of the words defined by context clues. On one side of the card write the word and the page number where you found it. At the top of the other side of the card, write the definition. At the bottom of the card write one example if the sentence includes examples. If the sentences does not include examples, think of an example yourself and write it at the bottom of the card.

EXERCISE 17

From a textbook you are reading for another course, find five sentences in which you are able to determine the meaning of a word from context. Write out each sentence and underline the word whose meaning you determined from context clues. Beneath the sentence write the meaning you deduced for the underlined word.

Summary

The meaning of a word is determined by its context. The sentence a word is in is the context of the word. Authors sometimes include clues in the sentence—the context of the word—that will help you decide on the meaning of a word.

When you come to a word you are unsure of, look first to see if the word has been defined directly by the author. Look for such words as "is defined," "means," or "is referred to." Check to make sure that you have found the definition by trying it in the formula "X means Y" where X stands for the word and Y stands for the definition. If the word is not defined directly, look for punctuation marks that may set off the word or its definition.

Words that are defined by the author directly or by punctuation context clues are often part of the technical or specialized vocabulary of the course in which the book is used. The word and its definition should be marked in the textbook. These words are important to know; a chart with the word, its definition, and an example can be used to organize the words in order to study them. Cards with the word on one side and the definition on the other will allow you to separate the words you know from the words that give you trouble.

Sometimes the meaning of an unfamiliar word can be deduced from the general sense of the sentence. By deciding what the sentence means, the reader can make an educated guess about what a word in the sentence might mean. In some cases a word is indirectly defined by contrasting it with a word in another part of the sentence or in the sentence that immediately precedes (comes before) it. Sometimes contrast signal words such as *however, but,* and *even though* may be used along with the general sense of the sentence to determine the meaning of a word.

It is not important that you know the names of the different types of context clues. What is important is that you are aware that context (the sentence) can sometimes be used to figure out the meaning of a word. Not every sentence will have context clues like punctuation or contrast signal words. Not every sentence will give enough information for you to make an educated guess about the meaning of a particular word in that sentence. However, you will often be able to use context to determine the meaning of an unfamiliar word and thus to make sense of the sentence. Using context clues is just one way to figure out unknown words. And it is the first way the good reader tries.

3 Word Parts

Take a look at this sentence:

Manley tried to circumvent the law whenever possible.

From this one sentence you might have trouble deciding whether or not Manley was a law-abiding citizen. However, if you happened to know that *circum* is a word part that means "around" and *ven* is a word part that means "come," then you could figure out that *circumvent* means "come around." In other words, Manley tried to get around the law whenever possible.

Now, granted, you would not have this single sentence about Manley in a textbook. This sentence would have been in a paragraph, and the context of that paragraph would have probably enabled you to make a decision about Manley's character. However, knowledge of the meaning of word parts and the ability to use that knowledge to figure out unknown words is another reading tool you can use. The more tools you can use, the more efficient a reader you will be.

Words are often made up of a *prefix*, a *combining form* (or root word), and a *suffix*. Take for example the word *incredible*.

prefix = in = not

combining form = cred = believe

suffix = ible = able

If you put the meaning of the parts together and rearrange them to make sense, you have "not able to believe."

Now try this one: *inaudible*. You need to know that *aud* means "hear."

So you have

    prefix   = in   = not

    combining form = aud = hear

    suffix   = ible = able

Put them together and you have "not able to hear."

If you look up *inaudible* in the dictionary, you might find its meaning given as "not audible." So then you would have to look up *audible*. Its meaning might be given as "heard or capable of being heard." So *inaudible* means "not heard or not capable of being heard." This is a more precise definition than we arrived at by looking at the meanings of the word parts. *Incredible* is defined in the dictionary as "too extraordinary and improbable to be believed, hard to believe"—again, a much more precise definition than ours.

However, remember that in your textbooks these words will be in sentences, and the context of the sentence plus your knowledge of word parts will get you close enough to the meaning of the word so that you can make sense of the sentence. Here are our two example words put into the context of a sentence.

Our seats at the concert were so far from the stage that the music was almost inaudible.

Many people find stories of alien life forms visiting earth incredible.

Did you have any trouble deciding that in the first sentence the music was hard to hear and in the second sentence the stories were hard to believe?

The point here is that to understand what you are reading, you must think about what you are reading; you must make sense of the message conveyed by the words. To do that you must not only know the meaning of the individual words but also the message communicated by those words.

Using word parts to understand the meaning of a word is a skill that you use along with context clues to figure out the meanings of unknown words. Knowing the meaning of the different parts of the word moves you close to the meaning of the word. Then that close meaning is made more precise by the context of the sentence in which the word appears.

Word Parts: Prefixes

A prefix is a word part that is added to the beginning of a word (called the base word) or a word part such as a combining form or root word. For example, the word *prefix* is made up of the prefix **pre** (before, in front) and the root word **fix** (to attach) and *prefix* means "to attach before or in front."

A prefix has a meaning and that meaning is added to the meaning of the base word, root word, or combining form to which it is attached. The prefix **dis** means "not." When **dis** is added to the base word *similar*, the word becomes *dissimilar* and means "not similar."

dis = not

dis + similar = not similar

That brings up a side benefit of knowing about prefixes; it can improve your spelling.

dis + similar = dis̲s̲imilar

There are two *s*'s in dissimilar because the first *s* belongs to the prefix **dis** and the second *s* belongs to the word *similar*. Let's try another example. **Mis** is a prefix that means "wrong or bad." If I want to write a word that means "spell wrong," I add **mis** to *spell* and get *misspell*.

mis + spell = mis̲s̲pell

You now know that this word is not spelled *mispell* because it has to have two *s*'s. One *s* belongs to the prefix **mis,** and the other *s* belongs to the word *spell*. Now you need never misspell *misspell* again.

Exercise 1 lists some common and useful prefixes. Some of these you may already know. Those you don't know you can look up in the dictionary. But be careful. For example, in addition to being a prefix, *post* can be a noun with several different meanings (a pole or stake, a soldier's station, a basketball position) or a verb also with different meanings (to affix to a usual place such as a wall, to ride with haste, to mail a letter, to assign to a location). Be sure you find the dictionary entry for *post* as a prefix. It will look something like this entry from Webster's *New Collegiate Dictionary.*

> **post-** *prefix* [ME, fr. L, fr. *post*; akin to Skt *paśca* behind, after, Gk *apo* away from — more at OF] **1 a** : after : subsequent : later <*post*date> **b** : behind : posterior : following after <*post*lude> **2 a** : subsequent to : later than <*post*operative> **b** : posterior to <*post*orbital>

Notice that this entry for *post* as a prefix has a hyphen (-) and the word *prefix* in italics. The first part of the entry is in brackets and gives information about the origin (the etymology) of the prefix. What you are looking for is the meaning of the prefix. There are several meanings, and they are numbered. Be sure to read all of them. Sometimes the meanings will be very similar. In that case you may select one to learn. On the other hand, you may find that the meanings are quite different. In that case you will need to know each different meaning. When trying to learn the meanings of prefixes, choose the most common meanings. You cannot learn all there is to know about prefixes, so choose to learn the most useful.

Notice also that you are given examples of a word with the prefix attached. These examples can come in handy when you are trying to learn the meanings of prefixes. However, the best example word is one you come up with on your own because it will be a word that you already know.

A very effective method of learning something new (like the meaning of the prefix **mis**) is to "hook" it or "anchor" it to something you already know (like the word *misspell*). When trying to learn that **mis** means "wrong," you might remember the example of *misspell*. You know that *misspell* means to "spell wrong" so you can remember that **mis** means "wrong."

Now let's examine in detail the entry for the prefix **post.** You do not need to remember all the details, but this information will help you in finding what you need to know when you look up prefixes in the dictionary.

> **post-** *prefix* [ME, fr. L, fr. *post*; akin to Skt *paśca* behind, after, Gk *apo* away from — more at OF] **1 a** : after : subsequent : later <*post*date> **b** : behind : posterior : following after <*post*lude> **2 a** : subsequent to : later than <*post*operative> **b** : posterior to <*post*orbital>

Let's see if we can sort all this out. For our purposes, we don't need to know the information in the brackets [ ]. This is information about the origin or the etymology of the word. For example, the "ME, fr. L." in the brackets tells us that the origin of the prefix **post** is from a Middle English word taken in turn from a Latin word.

What we need to know is the meaning of the prefix. Notice that the meanings are numbered **1a, b, 2a, b** and that the definitions are separated by a colon (:). Reading through all the definitions we see that *after, subsequent, later, behind, posterior, following after,* and *subsequent to* all carry the same core of meaning. So choose one definition from these to remember. Maybe "after" or "later."

Check out the examples: <*post*date>, <*post*lude>, <*post*operative>, <*post*orbital>. If one of the example words is already known to you, choose it as your "hook" or "anchor" to help you learn the meaning of *post*. If the examples are not familiar, come up with your own example. Maybe *postpone* (to put later or after).

Sometimes a prefix will have several different forms. For example, one meaning of the prefix **in** is "not." So if we would like to have a word that means "not legal," it would be *inlegal*. However, *inlegal* is hard to pronounce in English, so over the years the word has become *illegal*. Other examples of how **in** has changed its form are the following:

not regular = inregular = irregular

not possible = inpossible = impossible

Another prefix that changes its form is **com.** Study the following examples.

combine   connect   collect

Notice that all three words have a common core of meaning "together" or "with," which comes from the prefix **com.**

EXERCISE 1

This exercise gives a list of common prefixes. You are asked to decide on a definition and an example word for each. Space is provided for more than one meaning if a prefix has very different meanings. The first two are done for you, but you may want to come up with your own example word, one that you know well.

Prefix	Meaning	Example Word
1. anti	against	antisocial
2. ex	a. former	ex-husband
	b. out	exhale
3. dis	a. _____	_____
	b. _____	_____
4. inter	_____	_____
5. intra	_____	_____
6. post	_____	_____
7. pre	_____	_____
8. re	a. _____	_____
	b. _____	_____
9. mis	_____	_____
10. sub	_____	_____
11. super	_____	_____

12. in   a. _____   _____

             b. _____   _____

13. semi   _____   _____

14. de   a. _____   _____

             b. _____   _____

15. non   _____   _____

16. pro   a. _____   _____

             b. _____   _____

17. un   _____   _____

18. ad   _____   _____

19. hyper   _____   _____

20. mal   _____   _____

21. tele   _____   _____

22. pseudo   _____   _____

23. com, con, col   _____   _____

24. contra (sometimes shortened to con)   _____   _____

25. trans   _____   _____

EXERCISE 2

From the list in Exercise 1, list four prefixes that mean "not."

1. _____   **3.** _____

2. _____   **4.** _____

EXERCISE 3

Match the definition with the prefix in the columns below.

Prefix	Definition
_____ **1.** anti	a. opposite of
_____ **2.** dis	b. false
_____ **3.** ex	c. again
_____ **4.** re	d. distant
_____ **5.** pseudo	e. against
_____ **6.** tele	f. between
_____ **7.** semi	g. with, together
_____ **8.** inter	h. former, out of
_____ **9.** con	i. partly
_____ **10.** hyper	j. above, overly

EXERCISE 4

List twelve prefixes that give direction, location, or placement. By each prefix write its meaning. The first two are done for you.

1. ex – out of

2. inter – between

3. _____

4. _____

5. _____

6. _____

7. _____

8. _____

9. _____

10. _____

11. _____

12. _____

EXERCISE 5

Write the prefix that means the opposite of the prefix listed. In the blank by each prefix, write its definition. The first one is done for you.

Prefix	Definition	Prefix Meaning the Opposite	Definition
super	above	sub	under, below
post			
anti			
pro	forward		
in	in, inner		
ad			

EXERCISE 6

Fill in the blank with a word that *both* defines the prefix and makes sense in the sentence.

1. Jim is **anti**war. He is _____ the war.

2. The **pre**lude is performed _____ the service.

3. The **post**lude is performed _____ the service.

4. The **pre**ceding announcement is one that came _____.

5. A **re**ceding hairline is one that moves _____.

6. If a person is **mal**adjusted, he is adjusted _____.

7. To make **pro**gress is to move _____.

8. A **con**vocation is a time when people come _____.

9. A procedure that is **ir**regular is _____ regular.

10 An **inter**city bus travels _____ cities.

11. If a person is **dis**interested, she is _____ interested.

12. To **contra**vene a law is to go _____ it.

13. The **ex**it is the way _____.

14. To **mis**quote a person is to quote her _____.

15. The **sub**surface is the layer of rock right _____ the surface.

16. A **trans**atlantic flight goes _____ the Atlantic.

17. To **col**late pages is to put them _____ in order.

18. A **tele**meter measures _____.

19. A person who is **hyper**sensitive is _____ sensitive.

20. If a machine is **non**operational, it does _____ operate.

21. If a person is **de**moted, he is moved _____.

22. To be **semi**conscious is to be _____ conscious.

23. Astrology, which claims the future can be foretold by studying the stars, is considered to be a **pseudo**science; it is a _____ science because it is not based on accepted scientific principles.

24. If a person is **un**troubled, she is _____ troubled.

25. Rooms that are **ad**jacent are next _____ each other.

EXERCISE 7

Read the following paragraph, which is typical of one you might find in a psychology textbook. Then using both prefixes and context, define the underlined words in the space beneath the paragraph.

A person who has a lack of confidence in one area may find that other areas of his life are affected. For example, he may find that his attention is easily <u>distracted</u> when studying. He may not be able to meet deadlines for term papers and may not <u>interact</u> well with instructors or students. Although he may wear a face of confidence, it is <u>pseudobravery</u>. Others may think him <u>extroverted</u> and outgoing, whereas he is really an <u>introverted</u> person who is shy and timid. He may be <u>disapproving</u> and <u>hypercritical</u> of others, finding fault with the smallest, most trivial things—a trait others find <u>unattractive</u>. Instead of admitting his problems, he may <u>transpose</u> his fears to other people. For example, he may accuse a friend of <u>dissatisfaction</u> with their relationship when in reality he himself is the one who is <u>discontent</u>. He may even <u>descend</u> into a deep <u>depression</u> which he finds <u>insuperable</u>. In extreme cases, the person may become <u>nonfunctional</u>.

distracted _____

interact _____

pseudobravery _____

extroverted _____

introverted _____

disapproving _____

hypercritical _____

unattractive _____

transpose _____

dissatisfaction _____

discontent _____

descend _____

depression _____

insuperable _____

nonfunctional _____

Word Parts: Combining Forms

Root words and combining forms are word parts that are very useful to know because they can help you learn whole groups of words. For example:

somn	= sleep
in**somn**ia	= inability to sleep
somnolent	= sleepy
somnambulist	= one who sleep walks

As you can see from the above examples, the root word or combining form can be at the beginning or in the middle of the word. It can also be at the end of a word. For example:

vene	= come
con**vene**	= come together

The root **vene** comes from the Latin verb *venire*, which means "to come." Not all dictionaries will give the meaning of root words. However, most dictionaries do define combining forms. A combining form is a word part derived usually from a Greek or Latin word. In the dictionary a combining form has a dash and **comb form** (usually in italics) after it. It will look like this:

-logy *comb form* [ME *-logie*, fr. OF, fr. L *-logia*, fr. Gk, fr. *logos* word] **1** : oral or written expression <phraseo*logy*> **2** : doctrine : theory : science <ethno*logy*>

Once again we do not need to know the information about the etymology or origin of the combining form in the brackets. Notice the two meanings: (1) oral or written expression and (2) doctrine, theory, science. These two definitions are very different, and which definition you need will be determined by the context of the word (the sentence it is in).

You don't need to know whether a word part is a root word or a combining form. What is important is to realize that knowing the meanings of root words and combining forms will enable you to unlock the meanings of whole *groups* of words. For example, knowing that **cred** means "belief or trust" will help you figure out the following words:

credit	creditor	creditable	creditability
credible	incredible	credibility	incredibility
credulity	incredulity	credulous	incredulous
credentials	credence	creed	credo

Root words and combining forms may change their spelling as they are combined with other word parts. For example, from the Latin *mittere* we get **miss** as in the word *transmission* and **mit** as in the word *transmit*. We will treat **miss** and **mit** as different spellings of the same word part.

EXERCISE 8

In the following list of common root words and combining forms, you are asked to decide on a definition and come up with an example word. Only one root word (*path*) will have two meanings so different that you need to give two separate answers.

Root Word / Combining Form	Meaning	Example Word
aud	_____	_____
chron	_____	_____
cred	_____	_____
vert, vers	_____	_____
dict	_____	_____
graph	_____	_____
mit, miss	_____	_____
mort	_____	_____
ven, vene	_____	_____
phon	_____	_____
biblio	_____	_____
bio	_____	_____
gam, gamy	_____	_____
gyn	_____	_____
phobia	_____	_____
poly	_____	_____

vis, vid   _____   _____

port   _____   _____

duc, duct   _____   _____

gress   _____   _____

cede, ceed   _____   _____

path   a. _____   _____

            b. _____   _____

tract   _____   _____

spec   _____   _____

voc   _____   _____

EXERCISE 9

Match the word part with its correct definition in the columns below.

Word Part	**Definition**
_____ **1.** aud	a. turn
_____ **2.** chron	b. say, tell
_____ **3.** cred	c. hear
_____ **4.** vert	d. look, see
_____ **5.** dict	e. come
_____ **6.** graph	f. death
_____ **7.** spec	g. write
_____ **8.** ven	h. time
_____ **9.** mort	i. sound
_____ **10.** phon	j. believe

EXERCISE 10

Beside each statement write T if it is true or F if it is false. If the statement is false, mark out the incorrect word and write the correct word above it. The first one is done for you.

   _**F**_   **1.** *Bio* means ~~death~~. [*life* written above *death*]

_____   **2.** *Mort* means death.

_____   **3.** *Biblio* means bible.

_____   **4.** *Poly* means many.

_____   **5.** *Gress, cede, ceed* all mean stay.

_____   **6.** *Port* means carry.

_____   **7.** *Voc* means see.

_____   **8.** *Tract* means to draw.

_____   **9.** *Gyn* means marriage.

_____ **10.** *Vis* means see.

EXERCISE 11

Fill in the blank with a word that *both* defines the word part and makes sense in the sentence.

   1. A **gyn**ecologist treats _____ patients.

   2. A **port**able radio is one you can _____.

   3. A **vis**ionary is one who seems able to _____ into the future.

   4. A sym**path**etic person _____ the same as you do.

   5. A retro**spec**tive is a _____ backwards.

   6. A **biblio**graphy is a list of _____.

7. A trans**mit**tal form is _____ with another document.

8. **Polygamy** is the state of being _____ _____

   times.

9. If a story is **cred**ible, it can be _____.

10. If you **dic**tate a report, you _____ it.

11. If you in**vert** a bowl, you _____ it the opposite way.

12. To re**duce** is to _____ back or again to a former amount.

13. A pain that is **chron**ic is one you have all the _____.

14. A **bio**psy is a slice of _____ tissue.

15. A miso**gyn**ist is a person who hates _____.

16. Acro**phobia** is the _____ of high places.

17. A **mor**gue is a place where _____ bodies are placed.

18. To contra**dict** is to _____ against her.

19. To make pro**gress** is to _____ forward.

20. The **aud**io on the television is the part you _____.

21. The **vid**eo on the television is the part you _____.

22. The suc**ceed**ing page is the page that _____ after this one.

23. To auto**graph** a book is to _____ your name in your own

    hand.

24. To be at**tract**ed to a person is to be _____ to him or her.

25. **Path**ology is the study of _____.

Word Parts: Suffixes

A suffix is a word part that comes at the end of a word. Suffixes are not as useful in figuring out the meanings of words as prefixes and combining forms are. In the first place, many suffixes have the same or similar meaning. In the second place, the meanings of suffixes tend to be general and vague. In the third place, suffixes do not change the basic meaning of the word to which they are added but rather add their meaning to the base word. Below you will find a chart with common suffixes and their meanings.

State of, Condition of, Quality of	One Who	Full of	Relating to, Pertaining to
ance	er	ful	al
ence	or	ous	ic
tion	ist	ious	ish
ion			
ive			
ment			
ness			
ity, ty			
tude			

In the word *truthful*, the suffix is **ful** and the base word is *truth*. *Truthful* means "full of truth." As with prefixes, knowing about suffixes can help your spelling. Notice that the suffix is fu*l*, not fu*ll*. So now you know that *useful* is spelled with one *l* because you are adding to the base word *use* the suffix **ful.**

However, there is yet another problem with using suffixes to figure out unknown words. Take the word *reliance*. Break it into its parts. We know the suffix is **ance.** That leaves the rest of the word: "reli." Any idea what "reli" means? What if I tell you that the base word is *rely* and that the *y* is changed to an *i* before adding the suffix **ance.** Now that makes some sense because *relyance* would certainly look strange to us. So now if you know what *rely* means, you can figure out that *reliance* is the state, condition, or quality of relying. For many students that definition is so general as to be of little use. Furthermore, if you do not know what *rely* means, knowing the meaning of the suffix will not move you any closer to the meaning of the word.

Even though knowing suffixes is not as useful in figuring out the meaning of unknown words as knowing prefixes and root words, recognizing the most common suffixes is useful in helping you locate the root or base word. Take the following word.

changeable

This word might cause you to stumble. But if you take the suffix off, the word becomes immediately clear.

    change   able

The word must mean something like "able to change." Now try another one:

    measurability

At first this word may look totally unfamiliar. It actually has two suffixes. Let's take them off one at a time.

    measurabil   ity

Still look unfamiliar? Take the other suffix off.

    measur   abil   ity

Does "measur" remind you of the word *measure? Measure* is the base word; the final *e* was dropped before adding the first suffix. The word means something like "the quality of being able to be measured." The problem with this word is that you have to be able to recognize the word you are left with after you remove the two suffixes.

Because you are sometimes able to recognize a base word you know when you remove suffixes, knowing common suffixes can be useful. What you want to learn to do is to locate the base word by removing the suffix, remembering that the base word may have dropped an *e* or changed a *y* to *i*.

EXERCISE 12

See if you can locate the base word by removing the suffixes from the following words. Start at the end of the word and cover up the letters until you come to a word you recognize. If the base word ends in *i*, try changing the *i* to *y*. If the base word does not look familiar, try adding an *e* or a *y*. The first three are done for you.

	Suffix	**Base Word**
wishful	ful	wish
manageable	able	manage
defiance	ance	defy
allergic		
feverish		

electricity   _____   _____

dependence   _____   _____

readable   _____   _____

quietude   _____   _____

advisor   _____   _____

legality   _____   _____

resistance   _____   _____

cancerous   _____   _____

violation   _____   _____

musical   _____   _____

reddish   _____   _____

improvable   _____   _____

argument   _____   _____

maturity   _____   _____

plentiful   _____   _____

EXERCISE 13

Read the following passage, which is typical of one you might find in a health care textbook. Using your knowledge of prefixes, combining forms, and suffixes (as well as context clues), define the underlined words in the space below the passage.

As the number of older persons increases, the field of <u>gerontology</u> (the study of aging) has also grown. One problem of the elderly commanding attention is that of <u>sensory</u> loss such as failing <u>vision</u> and <u>auditory</u> ability. Changes in the sensory <u>acuity</u> or sharpness in the elderly are often mistaken for symptoms of disease or senility rather than the normal consequences of growing old, as <u>predictable</u> as gray hair and wrinkles.

Changes in taste and smell may lead to a <u>disinterest</u> in eating and in time to <u>malnutrition</u>. The <u>aromatic</u> appeal of foods is affected by a loss of the sense of smell. Older persons are more likely to describe the taste of food as weak or <u>nonexistent</u>. Older persons may not be able to smell a <u>pungent</u> odor such as ammonia or the <u>odorant</u> added to natural gas to make gas leaks <u>detectable</u>.

The sense of touch is also lessened as we grow older. Older persons react more slowly than do young people to <u>tactile</u> sensations such as heat and cold. Because older persons do not feel the cold as quickly, some may fall victim to <u>hypothermia</u>, <u>subnormal</u> temperature of the body.

The <u>prospect</u> of a progressive decline in our senses is <u>discomforting</u>, to say the least. However, the more we know about the problems of <u>diminished</u> senses, the more able we are to make them <u>bearable</u> by educating the elderly to compensate for failing senses and by providing safety measures in the home and other environments.

gerontology _____

sensory _____

vision _____

auditory _____

acuity _____

predictable _____

disinterest _____

malnutrition _____

aromatic _____

nonexistent _____

pungent _____

odorant _____

detectable _____

tactile _____

hypothermia _____

subnormal _____

prospect _____

discomforting _____

diminished _____

bearable _____

A Final Word About Figuring Out Unknown Words

Remember that using context clues and word parts are two very useful tools to help you unlock unknown words. There are two other skills you should employ. One is to try to sound out the word. The other is to use the dictionary. When you come to an unknown word, try the **CSSD** approach.

- **Context:** First try to figure out the word using context clues.

- **Sound:** If the context does not give you enough information to figure out the word, try to sound out the word. Sometimes when you pronounce the word, you will recognize it.

- **Structure:** If you can't pronounce the word or don't recognize it when you say it aloud, try breaking the word into parts (prefix, combining form, suffix) to see if you know the meaning of the parts. Then put the word back together using those meanings.

- **Dictionary:** Finally, if you still cannot figure out the word or if you want to check the accuracy of your guess about the meaning, go to the dictionary.

Many textbooks contain a **glossary,** which is a dictionary for that particular text; this will give the meaning of the specialized or technical words used in that text. Usually the glossary is at the end of the book. However, some texts have a word list with meanings at the end of each chapter. The index at the back of the book can also help you find meanings of technical words. Usually a technical word is defined when it is first used in the book. So look up the word in the index and then go to the first page listed for the word. You may find the definition given on that page.

A special note needs to be made about the skill of sounding out words. Some people are better at it than others. If you learned to read using the phonics method, you were taught the sounds letters make and the rules that govern those sounds. You may be quite good at pronouncing words. Good for you! You have a valuable and useful skill. Use it. Often when you sound out an unfamiliar word, you will recognize it. You may think "Oh, that is what that word is. I didn't know it was spelled that way, but now that I hear the word, I know what it is."

Unfortunately, others of you may not be so adept at pronouncing words. Maybe you were not taught the rules of phonics. Or maybe you were taught, but you don't remember them very well. Or maybe you just are not very good at it. If you are the type of person who cannot "carry a tune in a bucket," if you had trouble learning to play a musical instrument, if you don't learn well by listening, you may also not be able to sound words out well. Do not despair. Pronouncing the word may be helpful in recognizing it, but often it does not particularly help. Just keep in mind that there are other ways to figure out unknown words. It is not absolutely necessary that you be able to pronounce a word in order to make sense of the sentence in which the word appears.

On the other hand, if you are trying to learn new words in order to increase your vocabulary or because you must learn them for a course you are taking, you must be able to pronounce them. It is very difficult to remember words you cannot pronounce, and it is equally hard to remember how to spell them. In these special cases, you need to find someone who will help you learn the pronunciation of the words. Find out if your school has a learning center, a reading lab, or a place you can go for tutoring. If not, ask your reading instructor or find a classmate or a friend to help you. Ask the person to show you how to break the word apart. Have them pronounce each part as you look at it and then listen to you as you pronounce each part. Finally, practice saying the whole word aloud as you look at it.

4 Reading Sentences

Reading is the process used to understand a written message. The reader *receives* the message that the writer *sends*. Reading, then, is an act of communication between the writer and the reader. The responsibility of the writer is to convey (transmit or send) the message in as clear a manner as possible. The responsibility of the reader is to translate the message in as accurate a manner as possible.

In composition class or writing class you learn how to communicate clearly as a writer. The writing process is closely related to the reading process. The things you learn in composition about how to communicate clearly in writing can be used when you are trying to understand what someone else has written. As you work your way through this book, try always to relate what you learn about reading (receiving a written message) to what you have learned about writing (conveying a written message).

In composition class you may have discussed the importance of writing for a particular audience. The audience is those persons for whom a written message is intended. The style of writing and the vocabulary will be different for different audiences. For example, you would use a very simple style and vocabulary if you were writing to a five-year-old child. However, you would not use that same style and vocabulary if you were writing to someone your own age. Furthermore, you might use an altogether different style and vocabulary when writing to a potential employer.

College textbooks, of course, are written for a particular audience. The reader of a college text is assumed to be an adult with at least some high school education. The sophistication of the vocabulary and the complexity of the writing style are appropriate for such an audience. In addition, the writer may assume that the reader is familiar with certain concepts important to the field of study for which the textbook is written. For example, the author of a sociology text might assume that the reader understands such concepts as "culture" and "social structures."

Such assumptions plus the sophistication of the vocabulary and the complexity of the writing style may make textbooks hard to understand. Notice that I said "hard to understand" not "impossible to understand." We've already discussed ways of figuring out unfamiliar words. In the following chapters we will discuss how to find the message when the writing style is complex. We will begin with the sentence, the basic unit of a written communication.

Core Parts of a Sentence

You may remember from English or grammar classes that a sentence can be defined as a group of words expressing a complete thought. What the reader needs to do, of course, is to figure out what the thought or idea *is* that the sentence is expressing. The more the reader understands about how a sentence is structured, the easier it will be for him or her to comprehend (understand) sentences in college textbooks.

Every sentence has two core parts that express the essential thought or basic meaning of the sentence:

1. the part that tells who or what the sentence is about

2. the part that tells what is being said about the "who or what" of the sentence

In order to understand a sentence you must be able, then, to answer at least two basic questions:

1. **Who** or **what** is the sentence about?

2. **What is being said** about the "who or what" of the sentence?

Let's work with a simple sentence:

The student understands.

Who or what is this sentence about? *The student.* What is being said about the student? The student *understands.* The who or what of the sentence is called the **subject.** So in our example

The student understands.

the subject of the sentence is "the student." The part of the sentence that tells what is being said about the subject is the **predicate.** In our sentence the word *understands* is the predicate.

Let's take another simple sentence:

The teacher is happy.

Who or what is the sentence about? *The teacher.* The subject of this sentence is "the teacher." What is being said about the teacher? He (or she) *is happy.* So, "is happy" is the predicate.

Let's try one more example:

The cat ran up the tree.

Who or what is the sentence about? *The cat.* The subject is "the cat." What is being said about the cat? It *ran.* "Ran" is the predicate. The core parts of the sentence are "The cat ran."

Wait a minute! Maybe you thought that what was being said about the cat was that it "ran up the tree." Is that wrong? No. "Ran" is the simple predicate and "ran up the tree" is the complete predicate. Notice that the words "up the tree" just tell us more completely what is being said about the subject. "Ran up the tree" not only tells us *what* the cat did, it also tells us *where.* Look at this example:

About five o'clock Harry telephoned to find out why the store had not delivered the air conditioner he had bought that morning.

In the simplest terms the sentence is about Harry (the subject), and what is being said about Harry is that he telephoned (the simple predicate). Other parts of this sentence tell *when* he telephoned (about five o'clock) and *why* he telephoned (to find out why the store had not delivered the air conditioner he had bought that morning). But the basic meaning or essential thought of this sentence is "Harry telephoned."

Let's try one more example:

The boy bit the dog.

In this sentence the subject is "boy." The part that tells what is being said about the boy in the simplest terms is "bit." But isn't it natural to want to know who the boy bit? So in this sentence the core parts that express the basic meaning or essential thought are not only the subject (the boy) and the simple predicate (bit) but also the words that complete the meaning of the predicate (the dog).

The core parts of a sentence, then, are the words that express the basic meaning or essential thought of the sentence. You must be able to recognize the core parts of any sentence to understand it. You might remember from English or grammar classes that what we are calling the simple predicate is the verb in the sentence. In the sentence about the boy biting the dog, you might recognize that "dog" is the **direct object.** What we are calling the essential thought is the subject + the verb + the direct object (if there is one).

Now look at this sentence:

The boy had bitten the dog once before.

The subject is "the boy" but notice that the verb is "had bitten." The point here is that the verb may be made up of more than one word. "Had bitten" is called a verb phrase because it has more than one verb in it. "Had" is a verb and "bitten" is a verb, and together they make up the verb phrase "had bitten." What is important for you as a reader to notice about the verb phrase is that it is the last word in the verb phrase that carries the principal meaning. In our example of "had bitten," the last word is *bitten* and that is the word that carries the meaning of what is being said about the subject.

The last verb in a verb phrase is called the **main verb.** The other verbs in a verb phrase are called **auxiliary** (or helping) **verbs.** Check out the following examples in which the verb phrase has been underlined and note that in each case the last word in the verb phrase carries the meaning about what is being said about the boy.

The boy <u>is biting</u> his sister.

The boy <u>has been biting</u> for a long time.

The boy <u>can be helped</u>.

The boy <u>should have been helped</u> before now.

What you remember about the grammar of subjects and verbs and direct objects will help you in finding the essential thought of the sentence. However, if you don't remember very much, do not be concerned. We are not concerned here with grammar; we are concerned with sentence comprehension, and what is important in comprehending a sentence is that you can answer these questions:

1. Who or what is the sentence about? This is the subject.

2. What is being said about the subject? This is the predicate.

EXERCISE 1

In each of the following sentences locate the core parts that express the essential thought by drawing one line under the subject and two lines under the simple predicate. Keep the two basic questions in mind. The first one has been done for you.

1. On the Fourth of July at the park by the lake, many <u>people</u> <u>gathered</u> to watch the fireworks.

2. The library contains a copy machine.

3. The student should seek help as soon as he discovers he is falling behind.

4. The student had been registered for the course.

5. Harry concealed the letter in the bottom drawer of the chest beside his bed.

6. On the street behind the store the police discovered a discarded bag full of money.

7. In her lecture notes Mary had underlined the important details.

8. John has been making note cards to help him learn the definitions of important terms in his psychology class.

9. Sentences in textbooks can be long and complicated.

10. In a snow storm over the river and through the woods to grandmother's house by the frozen pond we go.

EXERCISE 2

The following sentences are typical of ones that might be found in a geology textbook. Locate the core parts that express the essential thought in each sentence by drawing one line under the simple subject and two lines under the simple predicate.

1. Geology is the study of the earth.

2. A major interest of the geologist is explaining the history of the earth through the study of rocks.

3. One geological method used to study the earth is making maps of the location of different rock types found at the surface of the earth.

4. Eight elements make up, for the most part, the crust—the outer few miles— of the earth.

5. Hardness is a property used to identify rocks.

Multiple Subjects and Verbs

Sometimes there may be more than one subject in a sentence. For example:

Jack and Jill went up the hill to fetch a pail of water.

The "who or what" this sentence is about is Jack *and* Jill. The two subjects are joined by the word *and*. Now you try the following sentence:

Hardness and color are properties used to identify rocks.

The subjects of this sentence are, of course, hardness and color. You may find that there are more than two subjects, as in the following sentence:

Hardness, color, luster, weight, taste, and radioactivity are among the properties used to identify rocks.

Here there are *six* subjects: hardness, color, luster, weight, taste, and radio-activity. Notice that the subjects are separated by a comma (,) and that the last two subjects are joined by *and*. There is no limit to the number of subjects a sentence can have. What is important for you as a reader is that you find *all* of the subjects.

Now study the following sentence:

Jack sang and danced.

Only one subject (Jack) but there are two verbs (sang and danced). So a sentence can have two or more subjects and two or more verbs. Again, what is important for you as a reader is to find *all* of the subjects and *all* of the verbs in the essential thought. Try the following sentence:

Venus and Mars can be seen by telescope and thus have been carefully studied.

The essential thought of this sentence is

Venus and Mars can be seen and have been studied.

EXERCISE 3

The following sentences have multiple subjects and verbs. Draw a line under the words that express the essential thought of the sentence.

1. The library and the bookstore contain copy machines.

2. The student should seek help as soon as he discovers he is falling behind and follow the advice he receives.

3. Harry and Daniel discovered the letter in the bottom drawer of the chest.

4. Math and science courses are often taken in the summer session by students who wish to be able to concentrate on one subject.

5. Earthquakes and glaciers are studied by geologists.

6. College textbooks may contain unfamiliar words and long, complicated sentences and can be confusing to read.

7. Alcohol and cigarettes are physically addictive and are also psychologically addictive.

8. Many changes and improvements have been made in computers over the years.

9. The computer can be used by doctors to aid in diagnoses and can help pharmacists keep track of drug prescriptions.

10. Some drugs should not be taken with other drugs and may cause a severe reaction.

Are you ready to find the essential thought of a very long, very complicated sentence? Try this one:

> After the morning ball game and before the evening campfire, Jack and Jill went slowly up the hill and fetched a large pail of cool and clean water to be used in cooking the meal for the family reunion to be held that afternoon at the park by the lake where many people watched fireworks on the Fourth of July.

The essential thought is "Jack and Jill went and fetched a pail." The rest of the sentence tells more about when, where, why, and how they went and more about the pail they fetched. So you can see that in addition to the essential thought a sentence will have parts that might answer such questions as

- When?

- How?

- Why?

- Where?

EXERCISE 4

In the following exercise use words from the sentences to answer the questions after each sentence. The first two are done for you.

1. In the nineteenth century, industrialization changed society forever.

   a. Essential thought? <u>Industrialization changed society</u>

   b. When? <u>In the nineteenth century</u>

   c. For how long? <u>Forever</u>

2. Human beings have the ability to communicate through language.

   a. Essential thought? <u>Human beings have the ability</u>

   b. What ability? <u>To communicate through language</u>

3. Language allows humans to share in the experiences of those who lived before.

   a. Essential thought? _____

   b. What are humans allowed to share in? _____

   c. Whose experiences are humans allowed to share in? _____

   _____

4. Because they can record and store information, humans are able to build on past knowledge.

   a. Essential thought? _____

   b. What can humans build on? _____

   c. Why can humans build on past knowledge? _____

   _____

5. Graphite is made up of carbon layers stacked one on top of the other.

   a. Essential thought? _____

   b. What is graphite made up of? _____

   c. What words describe the carbon layers? _____

Finding More Than One Essential Thought

Study the following sentence:

> Parents know that commercials are sometimes exaggerated, but children often believe everything they see.

In this sentence that are *two* essential thoughts:

1. parents know
2. children believe

The two essential thoughts are separated by a comma (,) and by the word *but*. Other words that are used to separate two essential thoughts are

> for   nor   yet
>
> and   or   so

These words are **coordinating conjunctions.** For our purposes what is important is that when we see one of these words with a comma, look for *two* essential thoughts. Try another example:

> The planet Mars is farther away from the sun, so it has a lower temperature than Earth.

The coordinating conjunction or joining word is *so*. The two essential thoughts are

1. the planet Mars is farther away
2. it has a lower temperature

Sentences that have two essential thoughts joined by a coordinating conjunction are called **compound sentences.** Remember that a coordinating conjunction plus a comma signal the reader to look for two essential thoughts. It will help if you draw a box around the comma and the coordinating conjunction to remind yourself to find the two essential thoughts as in the following sentence:

> In college courses lectures provide very important information, yet some
>
> students do not take notes during a lecture.

The two essential thoughts are "lectures provide very important information" and "some students do not take notes."

A special note must be made about the joining word *nor*. Something strange happens when you separate two essential thoughts joined by *nor*. Take the following sentence for example:

John did not pass math, nor did he pass English.

If you simply separate the two essential thoughts you get:

1. John did not pass math

2. did he pass English

What the sentence means, of course, is "John did not pass math, and he did not pass English." Notice that to make sense of the second essential thought you have to rearrange the subject and the verb and add *not*. Reading is a thinking activity. When you see a comma plus *nor*, you know you have two essential thoughts. However, you also have to think about what the second idea means. You have to replace *nor* with *and* and add *not*. Now try translating the following sentence into the two essential thoughts that it expresses.

Reading textbooks is not easy, nor is it impossible.

The two essential thoughts are "reading textbooks is not easy" and "reading textbooks is not impossible." Remember that it is not enough simply to find the two essential thoughts in a compound sentence with *nor*. You must make sense of what the second essential thought means.

EXERCISE 5

In the space following each of the following sentences, write the two essential thoughts of the sentence.

1. I do not like math, nor do I care for science.

Essential thought 1: _____

Essential thought 2: _____

2. Marsha has not decided what courses to take next semester, nor has she made an appointment with her advisor.

Essential thought 1: _____

Essential thought 2: _____

3. John does not expect to fail algebra, nor does he expect to pass chemistry.

Essential thought 1: _____

Essential thought 2: _____

4. Evan does not intend to miss class, nor does he mean to be late to class.

Essential thought 1: _____

Essential thought 2: _____

5. Studying is not the same process as reading, nor is it the same process as memorization.

Essential thought 1: _____

Essential thought 2: _____

When you mark the essential ideas in a sentence, try to underline just the key words that express the basic meaning. By underlining only key words, you will be a more active reader because you must think about what the sentence means. You cannot choose which words in the sentence to underline without thinking about what the basic meaning of the sentence is. Here are two examples of key word underlining:

<u>Reading</u> is <u>not</u> an <u>easy</u> process, but it <u>is</u> a <u>necessary</u> one for <u>success</u> in <u>college</u>.

Some <u>students</u> do <u>not know how</u> to <u>study</u>, <u>nor</u> do they know <u>where</u> to <u>get help</u>.

EXERCISE 6

Underline the key words that express the two essential thoughts in each of the following sentences.

1. Reading is the process used to understand a written message, and studying is the process used to remember the information.

2. Reading is not the same process as studying, but many students just read material they want to remember.

3. Some students read the information many times, yet they cannot remember it.

4. Rereading material does not ensure that it will be remembered, nor is it an efficient way to study.

5. Saying information out loud is a good way to study, or writing the information in your own words can be helpful.

6. Some students make note cards, and they practice saying the information on the note cards out loud.

7. A test will often determine your grade, so studying information that will be on the test is important.

8. Instructors may tell you information to study, or you can ask questions about what to study.

9. You should not ask a general question like "What will be on the test?" but you should ask a specific question like "Should we be able to label the parts of a cell?"

10. Studying is not easy, nor should it be postponed until the night before the test.

Finding the More Important Thought

Sometimes a sentence will have two thoughts or ideas, but one is more important than the other. For example:

> Even though much research has been done on sleep, no one knows for sure why we sleep.

The two parts of the sentence are:

1. even though much research has been done on sleep

2. no one knows for sure why we sleep

This sentence expresses two thoughts:

1. much research has been done on sleep

2. no one knows for sure why we sleep

Thought 2 is more important than thought 1. The author has made this clear by using the words *even though* and setting off thought 1 by a comma. "Even though much research has been done on sleep" is called a **dependent clause** because it doesn't make sense by itself but depends on the rest of the sentence to make sense. "No one knows for sure why we sleep" *does* make sense by itself and is called an **independent clause.** What is important for reading comprehension is that you recognize that there are two thoughts and that one is more important. Remember, the less important thought does not make sense when read all by itself. The more important thought does. Try this example:

> No one can do without sleep entirely for an unlimited amount of time although people are adaptable with regard to how much sleep they need.

The two parts of the sentence are:

1. no one can do without sleep entirely for an unlimited time

2. although people are adaptable with regard to how much sleep they need

Which thought is more important? The first one. This time the less important thought is not set off by a comma, but it is introduced with the word *although.* If I read the second thought all by itself

> although people are adaptable with regard to how much sleep they need

it seems incomplete. That is because it is a dependent clause and depends on the rest of the sentence to make sense. Sentences with an independent clause and a dependent clause are called **complex sentences.** What is important for the reader is to recognize that two thoughts are expressed and that one thought is more important than the other. The other thought is not unimportant; it is just less important.

The following words are often used to introduce less important thoughts:

after	that	when	which
although	whenever	once	since
as	so that	because	until
even though	if	unless	whereas
before	though	while	who

EXERCISE 7

In the following sentences draw a line under the more important thought.

1. Because it contains caffeine, a cup of coffee can raise your heart and breathing rates and your blood pressure.

2. Coffee can irritate the stomach lining if it is taken on an empty stomach.

3. Even though coffee can stimulate you mentally and physically, large doses can make you restless and jittery.

4. Although questions have been raised concerning the effect of caffeine on the developing fetus, no association has been established between the pregnant woman's intake of coffee and effects on the baby.

5. While some of the official programs report impressive success rates, many people break the smoking habit on their own.

6. Once nicotine is withdrawn, the person may experience irritability, depression, and anxiety, as you know only too well if you've ever tried to stop smoking.

7. Since smoking is psychologically addictive, you must first have the desire to quit.

8. You should substitute a physical activity such as taking a short walk whenever you feel the urge to smoke.

9. Some people brush their teeth when they want a cigarette because brushing freshens the mouth so that the urge to smoke is decreased.

10. After you quit smoking, you will be surprised that you ever wanted to smoke.

Reading Punctuation

Punctuation marks are sometimes overlooked by students as they read. The result is often a misunderstanding of the sentence. Although they are small, punctuation marks are big when it comes to sentence comprehension. For example, notice how just one comma can change the meaning of a sentence.

1. After we finished eating, Harry, Gail, Susan, and I went for a walk.
   Meaning: First we ate and then the four of us went for a walk.

2. After we finished eating Harry, Gail, Susan, and I went for a walk.
   Meaning: First we ate Harry, then the three of us went for a walk.

One of the most important punctuation marks for reading comprehension is the semicolon (;). The semicolon is used to separate two independent but closely related sentences. For example:

A person who lets someone else copy his test paper may not consider himself to be cheating; however, both persons are participating in the cheating and may be failed.

There are two essential thoughts here:

1. a person may not consider himself to be cheating

2. both persons are participating and may be failed

The semicolon serves as a stop sign to signal that one thought has been completed. In this sentence, the word *however* serves as a contrast word to signal a different but equally important thought. Other contrast words or phrases used in this way are the following:

nevertheless	on the contrary	in a different manner
on the other hand	instead	otherwise

Another important punctuation mark for reading comprehension is the colon (:). For our purposes, the thing to know about the colon is that it is often used to introduce a list whereas a comma will separate the items in the list. For example:

Heavy drinking during pregnancy can produce fetal alcohol syndrome, which can cause the following: retarded growth, low intelligence, and poor motor development.

If groups of things are listed, commas are used to separate the things in each group. In that case a semicolon will be used to separate the groups.

Cigarette smoking has been linked to the following: cancer of the lung, esophagus, larynx, and mouth; heart disease; shortness of breath, emphysema, and other breathing problems.

An author sometimes will include information that is interesting but not necessary to the essential thought of the sentence. This information will most often be set off by commas, dashes, or parentheses.

Amphetamines—often called uppers or speed—used to be available without a prescription.

Dieters take amphetamines to suppress the appetite (which they do for a short time).

Sleep disorders, nightmares for example, are often the result of stress.

EXERCISE 8

The purpose of this exercise is to make you more aware of the role punctuation plays in reading comprehension. There are two sentences in each set. The words are the same in each sentence, but the punctuation is different. Therefore, the meaning of the two sentences in each set is different. Read the two sentences in each set very carefully, noting the punctuation. Then answer the questions that follow each set.

Set 1   A. When the lightning struck Mary, James fainted.

B. When the lightning struck, Mary James fainted.

1. In sentence A, who fainted? _____

2. In sentence B, who fainted? _____

Set 2   A. Mr. Jones asked to see Jim and then called in Bill; the captain of our team, Joe, said he thought we were next.

B. Mr. Jones asked to see Jim and then called in Bill, the captain of our team; Joe said he thought we were next.

1. In sentence A, who is the captain of the team? _____

2. In sentence B, who is the captain of the team? _____

Set 3   A. When I saw Janet, she said she would call you in the morning; I will check with you to see if she did.

B. When I saw Janet, she said she would call you; in the morning I will check with you to see if she did.

1. In sentence A, what can you expect to happen in the morning?_____

_____

2. In sentence B, what can you expect to happen in the morning?_____

_____

Set 4   A. When I looked into the room, I saw Mary seated at the desk; Jim was at work on the computer and did not hear me call.

B. When I looked into the room, I saw Mary; seated at the desk, Jim was at work on the computer and did not hear me call.

1. In sentence A, who was seated at the desk? _____

2. In sentence B, who was seated at the desk? _____

Set 5   A. It is the experience of playing, and not winning, that counts.

B. It is the experience of playing and not winning that counts.

1. In sentence A, what is the experience that counts? _____

_____

2. In sentence B, what is the experience that counts? _____

_____

Set 6   A. You should consider the expense, the priority factor (the time involved), and the value of the experience.

B. You should consider the expense, the priority factor, the time involved, and the value of the experience.

1. In sentence A, how many things should you consider? _____

2. List the things to consider in sentence A. _____

_____

3. In sentence B, how many things should you consider? _____

4. List the things to consider in sentence B. _____

_____

Set 7   A. Integrating sensory input is the function of the parietal lobes located at the middle of the brain; the somatosensory cortex receives information from the skin senses and muscles.

B. Integrating sensory input is the function of the parietal lobes; located at the middle of the brain, the somatosensory cortex receives information from the skin senses and muscles.

1. In sentence A, what is located at the middle of the brain? _____

   _____

2. In sentence B, what is located at the middle of the brain? _____

   _____

Set 8

A. The treaty was signed by three nations involved in the border dispute in 1956; one nation refused to abide by all agreements, however, and the battles began once again.

B. The treaty was signed by three nations involved in the border dispute; in 1956 one nation refused to abide by all agreements, however, and the battles began once again.

1. In sentence A, what happened in 1956? _____

2. In sentence B, what happened in 1956? _____

Set 9

A. A few weeks before the cease fire began, the peace talks were moved to a new location; the final border disputes were settled and conditions of surrender finalized a month later.

B. A few weeks before, the cease fire began; the peace talks were moved to a new location, the final border disputes were settled and conditions of surrender finalized a month later.

1. In sentence A, when were the peace talks moved? _____

2. In sentence B, when were the peace talks moved? _____

Set 10

A. There should be a committee made up of the following: the president of the college, a professor of English, math, or one of the technologies, a psychologist, a physician, a counselor or a minister.

B. There should be a committee made up of the following: the president of the college; a professor of English, math, or one of the technologies; a psychologist, a physician, a counselor, or a minister.

1. In sentence A, how many people should be on the committee? _____

   _____

2. In sentence B, how many people should be on the committee? _____

EXERCISE 9

The following passage, taken from an introductory philosophy textbook, discusses the beliefs of the ancient Greeks.[1] Underline the words that express the essential thought in each sentence.

It was believed, first, that the world initially was in a state of chaos, but that some god, or gods, brought cosmos or order out of the chaos by fashioning the earth, the sun, the stars, and so forth. Second, they believed that the natural world, now so secured, was just, fair, and equitable, and would continue to be so as long as each god (who was given a different portion of the universe to rule over) refrained from upsetting the balance by overstepping the boundary of some other god's territory. But third, they believed that strife and tension were present along with order. However, this tension and conflict (as between such opposing forces as Night and Day, Winter and Summer, Love and Hatred) never went too far, with one force permanently rising triumphant over the other. Were that to happen, the balance would be upset and chaos would again set in. They were certain, however, that that would never happen again. They believed, finally, that the world, so fashioned and so sustained, was composed of four different kinds of stuff (or elements, as they were later called): earth, air, fire, and water.

Qualifying Words

Little words can make a big difference in understanding sentences. You can easily see that difference when the qualifying words *all*, *some*, or *none* are used. You will often find these qualifying words in test questions, and unless you are careful to pay attention to them, you may mistake the meaning of the questions. Now look at the following examples and note how one word can change the meaning of the sentence.

1. *All* of the ten questions will be graded.

2. *Some* of the ten questions will be graded.

3. *None* of the ten questions will be graded.

Sentence 1 means that *each and every* question without exception will be graded. Sentence 2 means that *at least one and maybe up to nine* questions will be graded. Sentence 3 means that *not a single one* of the questions will be graded.

The word *since* can mean "because," or it can be used to indicate a period of time. Note the following examples:

1. Paul had wanted to be a doctor since he was a little boy.

2. Paul wanted to be a doctor since his father was one.

Since in sentence 1 indicates the period of time that Paul has wanted to be a doctor (from the time that he was a little boy). In sentence 2, *since* is used in the sense of "because" and indicates a *reason* for Paul's wanting to be a doctor (his father was one). However, study the following sentence:

Since his father died during surgery, Paul has considered becoming a doctor.

In this sentence is *since* used to indicate a reason or to indicate a period of time? Actually it could be either. His father's death could be a reason for Paul's wanting to become a doctor or it could be that ever since the time that his father died, Paul has wanted to become a doctor. You would have to depend on the context of the paragraph to know how the word *since* is used here. The important thing for reading comprehension is to know the two senses the word *since* can have and to be alert to which sense is meant.

The word *as* can also indicate a time period or a reason. Sometimes it means "at the same time" as in this example:

Answer the questions as you read the chapter.

This sentence means that during the time that you are reading the chapter, you should also answer the questions. But sometimes the word *as* indicates a reason:

I took math in the summer session as I wanted to get my math requirements out of the way.

In this example you could substitute the word *because* for the word *as* and not change the sense of the sentence.

The small word *if* is a very important word. The words that follow *if* state a condition. Look at this example:

If it rains, the picnic will be cancelled.

The words following *if* (it rains) set a condition for cancellation of the picnic. If the condition set in the "if" part of the sentence is met, then the rest of the sentence is true or will happen. So if the condition of raining is met, then the picnic will be cancelled. This is a very important concept to master, particularly in computer programming and in the sciences. For example, look at this next sentence, which might appear in the directions for a chemistry experiment.

If the first mixture has become clear, add the second one to it.

Now you are to add the second mixture to the first. However, there is a condition that has been set: The first mixture has to become clear. What this sentence means, then, is first the condition of the first mixture being clear must be met and then the second mixture is to be added. What would happen if you added the second mixture *before* the first has become clear? We are not sure. Perhaps disaster! So, for reading comprehension the important thing to know about the word *if* is that the words following it set a condition that must be met before the rest of the sentence is true or should happen.

If you pass English 101, then you can take English 201.

What is the condition set for taking English 201? First you pass English 101. Another word that is important for reading comprehension is the word *unless*. One way to translate *unless* is "but not if."

We will have a picnic unless it rains.

We will have a picnic but not if it rains.

Now this is a little tricky because the condition being set for having a picnic is *not* that it rains. You might think that "it rains" is the condition set for having the picnic because we have just said that the words that follow *if* set a condition. However, in this sentence because the word *unless* means "but not if," the condition set is that it *not* rain. In other words, the condition set by the word *unless* is the negative of the words that follow *unless*. Try this sentence:

I will buy a car unless I get a raise.

What is the condition for my buying a car? *Not* getting a raise. Does that sound suspicious? Read the sentence again carefully. What it means is

I will buy a car but not if I get a raise.

I will buy a car if I don't get a raise.

Read these sentences over until you understand them. The concept of *unless* meaning "but not if" is sometimes confusing but always important. The formula is this:

X unless Y

X but not if Y

X if not Y

EXERCISE 10

The following exercise will make you more aware of the importance of qualifying words. There are two sentences in each set. Read each sentence, paying careful attention to the qualifying words. Then answer the questions following each set.

Set 1 A. Add the second mixture when the first has become clear.

B. Add the second mixture unless the first has become clear.

1. Which sentence indicates that you may *not* want to add the second mixture?

_____

2. When would you *not* add the second mixture? _____

_____

Set 2 A. The prescribed medication may be given if the patient is under the supervision of a doctor.

B. The prescribed medication may be given when the patient is under the supervision of a doctor.

1. Which sentence sets a condition for giving the medication? _____

_____

2. What is the condition that must be met before the medication can be given?

_____

Set 3　　A. Do not answer question 5 until you answer question 3.

B. Do not answer question 5 if you answered question 3.

1. Which sentence indicates that you must answer both questions? _____

_____

2. Which question must be answered first? _____

Set 4　　A. Some of the sections in Chapter 10 will be assigned.

B. None of the sections in Chapter 10 will be assigned.

1. Which sentence indicates that you will not be assigned Chapter 10?

_____

Set 5　　A. After you read the chapter, underline all the important facts.

B. As you read the chapter underline all the important facts.

1. Which sentence indicates that you read the entire chapter first before

underlining anything? _____

Set 6　　A. The treaty will not be ratified since Iran will not agree to the fifth article.

B. The treaty will not be ratified unless Iran agrees to the fifth article.

1. Which sentence indicates that Iran has decided *not* to agree to the fifth

article? _____

2. Which sentence indicates a reason for the treaty not being ratified?

_____

3. Which sentence sets a condition for the ratification of the treaty?

_____

4. What is the condition set for ratifying the treaty? _____

_____

Set 7   A. If the bell rings, you must stop the experiment.

B. When the bell rings, you must stop the experiment.

1. Which sentence indicates that during the experiment the bell will ring?

_____

2. Which sentence sets a condition for stopping the experiment?_____

_____

3. What is the condition set for stopping the experiment? _____

_____

Set 8   A. Lever C must be down when the switch connects.

B. Lever C must be down since the switch connects.

1. Which sentence gives a reason for lever C being down? _____

2. What is the reason that lever C is down? _____

Set 9   A. You will need to take that course if you graduate.

B. You will need to take that course before you graduate.

1. Which sentence indicates that first you graduate and then you take the

course? _____

Set 10   A. I understood how to do the problem before I read the chapter.

B. I understood how to do the problem as I read the chapter.

1. Which sentence indicates that reading the chapter was not necessary for

me to understand the problem? _____

Summary

Because reading is the process used to receive the written message that the author sends, reading is an act of communication. The responsibility of the reader is to decode or translate the author's message in as accurate a way as is possible. To do this, the reader must actively try to make sense of the written message by thinking about what the author is saying.

Reading and writing are closely related processes. What has been learned about how to communicate clearly in writing can be used to understand what another person has written. The more the reader understands about the structure of a sentence, the basic unit of communication, the more accurately he or she is able to decode a written message.

The core parts of a sentence are those words that express the basic or essential thought of the sentence. The core parts of a sentence are the subject plus the simple predicate. The two basic questions that must be answered to understand the essential thought of a sentence are "Who or what is the sentence about?" and "What is being said about the who or what that the sentence is about?"

A sentence may have several subjects and several verbs. The reader must be sure to find all the subjects and all the verbs that express the essential thought of the sentence.

A compound sentence may have more than one essential thought. The semicolon is used to separate the two essential thoughts in a compound sentence. A complex sentence has two thoughts and one is more important than the other. The more important thought in a complex sentence is in the independent clause, the clause that makes sense when read by itself.

Punctuation is used by writers to make their message clear. Reading comprehension is improved when readers understand the functions of different punctuation marks.

Small words can play a big role in the meaning of a sentence. The reader should be aware that some words have different meanings. For example, the word *since* can mean "because," or it can indicate a period of time. Qualifying words such as *all* and *none* are very important and should be noted by the reader. The words *if* and *unless* both signal that a condition has been set.

Textbooks may take effort to understand because of the sophistication of the writing style. The active reader is alert to punctuation and qualifying words. Reading comprehension is also enhanced (improved) by understanding the structure of sentences and using that understanding to find the core parts that express the essential thought of a sentence.

5 Reading Written Directions

Ever put together a new lawn mower following the enclosed set of instructions and have three screws and four washers left over? Ever try to sew a dress from a pattern only to have the zipper end up on the wrong side? Being able to follow written directions can make the difference between a lawn mower that works and one that falls apart or a dress that you would be proud to wear and one that is only fit for the rag bag. Not being able to follow directions can cost you money.

In college, not following directions can cost you a good grade. Ever lose points on a test because you didn't follow the instructions? Ever receive a low grade on a project because it wasn't done according to the instructor's directions? Did you ever do the wrong assignment, turn an assignment in late, or not do an assignment because you did not understand the directions?

In some of your courses like computer programming, accounting, data processing, secretarial science, construction, electrical and mechanical technology, much of your textbook reading will be reading to understand written directions. Even if you are not taking courses such as these, almost every day in college you will have to be able to read and follow directions. Some instructors say that the ability to read and follow written directions is the most valuable skill a college student can have. Because this reading skill is so essential, we have devoted an entire chapter to learning how to read written directions.

Core Parts

The first thing to notice about written directions is the type of sentence that is used. Often the subject (the who or what the sentence is about) is *you*, the reader. When the subject is you, the reader, the word *you* is not included in the sentence. In this case, the subject is said to be understood. Take the following sentence, for example:

Shut the door.

Who or what is this sentence about? You, the reader. If this sentence had the subject written out it would look like this:

You shut the door.

This type of sentence is called an **imperative sentence** because it issues a command or gives an order. The word *imperative* is defined as "a command or order" and "a rule or guide." In such sentences the subject is understood to be "you."

Because the subject is not written out but is understood, imperative sentences begin with a verb and almost always include a direct object, a word that receives the action of the verb. In our example above, the direct object is "the door." One way to figure out the direct object is to ask a question made up of the verb in the sentence and the words "who or what." So, in our example, the question would be "Shut who or what?" The answer to the question (the door) is the direct object. The core parts or essential thought of an imperative sentence is the verb plus the direct object. Try another example:

Circle the letter of the correct answer.

Find the verb by asking "What should I do?" Answer: circle. Find the direct object by asking "Circle what?" Answer: the letter. In this sentence, the essential thought is "circle the letter." The rest of the sentence describes the letter to be circled.

Notice in our sentence that the essential thought, "circle the letter," doesn't tell us all we need to know in order to be able to follow the directions correctly. We also need to know which letter to circle, and the rest of the sentence gives us that information. When reading directions, finding the essential thought is a start, but remember that the essential thought may not tell you all you need to know.

Let's try one more example:

Underline the word that is not correct.

What should you do? Underline. Underline what? The word. What word? The word that is not correct. In this sentence, as in many written directions, every word is important. You should get into the habit of underlining the essential thought plus other key words in written directions. For instance you might underline our last example in this manner:

<u>Underline</u> the <u>word</u> that is <u>not</u> <u>correct</u>.

Notice that the underlined words carry the message of the sentence: underline word not correct. You should underline the key words in sentences that give directions including the directions on a test you are taking. If you don't know if you are allowed to write on the test, ask the instructor.

EXERCISE 1

Underline the key words in the following sentences.

1. Make a study schedule that is workable.

2. Draw a chart with the days of the week and the hours in each day marked off.

3. Fill in the hours that you are in class.

4. Then fill in the hours that you are engaged in other activities such as hours you are at work, time set aside for preparing meals, times when you want to watch a favorite television program.

5. From the hours that are left, fill in the hours that are best for you to study.

6. Try to allow at least two hours of study for each hour in class even if you don't think you need that much time to study.

7. If you cannot find enough study time, rethink your school schedule because you may be trying to take too many courses.

8. If you cannot cut down on the number of courses you are taking, analyze your work and home responsibilities.

9. Cut down on the number of hours you are working if possible.

10. Decide which of your home responsibilities can be reassigned to someone else in the family, for example grocery shopping.

Signal Words

Remember that reading a set of directions calls for careful reading. You must pay attention to punctuation and to important qualifying words. Often you will be given signal words that tell you the order you are to do each step in the directions. Get into the habit of drawing a box around these signal words to make them stand out. Notice how the following set of directions has been marked.

When given a set of instructions to follow $\boxed{\text{first}}$ read the entire set to get a general idea of what you are being asked to do. $\boxed{\text{Next}}$ underline the essential thought plus key words in each step and be alert for qualifying words. $\boxed{\text{Then}}$ go back and number each step. $\boxed{\text{Finally}}$, check off each step as you complete it.

The following is a list of signal words that authors often use to point out the steps in a set of directions.

first	in addition	as	finally
then	second	before	equally important
following	last	moreover	furthermore
when	next	also	

In composition or writing class, what we are calling **signal words** are sometimes called **transition words, transitional markers,** or **transitionals.** The function of a signal word is to help the reader follow the thought that the author is expressing. In the case of directions, what the author is telling the reader is a certain process (how to do something). The signal words point out the steps in the process and tell the reader the order in which the steps are to be done.

Of course, not each and every step will be signalled by a signal word. Keep in mind that reading is a thinking activity. As you read through the steps, number each step as you come to it. Try to visualize yourself actually performing each step. Try to see the logic in the sequence of the steps by thinking about how one step leads to another. As you read through the steps, ask yourself why each step must be completed before the next one. After you have read the directions, try to repeat them to yourself and then check to see if you left any steps out. To check your understanding of the directions, quickly list the steps in order. You don't have to write out each step completely; you can just write down the key words of each step.

Following these suggestions will help you become an active reader. The more active you are in the reading process, the better your comprehension will be. On the other hand, if you simply read the directions through without thinking about them, you will be a passive reader, and your comprehension will not be as good. You know how easy it is to lose your concentration when you read. That often happens to passive readers. However, the active reader who combines reading and thinking will be better able to concentrate.

Think about it for a moment. Why do you lose your concentration? Isn't it because you start thinking about something else? If you are thinking about your reading, then you cannot think about something else, so you can't lose your concentration. If you are sitting in the stands watching a tennis match (a passive activity), you might start to daydream. However, if you are on the court playing in the match (active participation), it is very unlikely that you will start to daydream.

EXERCISE 2

Mark the following sets of directions by drawing a box around signal words and underlining essential thoughts and key words. Each set has a short introduction to help you put the directions into context. Be sure to read the introduction so that you can more easily understand the set of directions.

Set 1   These directions are typical of those that might be found in a textbook on child care; they explain how to respond to medical emergencies that might occur when a child is under your care.

If you discover a child has eaten or drunk a poisonous household cleaning product, you must act very quickly to save her life. First, call the ambulance and tell the attendant what has happened. Then, as you wait for the ambulance, cover the child with a warm blanket. Finally, be sure to take the product that the child has ingested with you to the hospital.

Set 2   These instructions from a fundamentals of nursing textbook describe one of the responsibilities of a nurse: assisting a patient to move in bed. Patients will require different levels of assistance. For example, the elderly patient recovering from surgery will require more help than will a young, healthy woman after giving birth.[1]

How then does the nurse determine what the client is able to do alone and how many people are needed to help move the client in bed? First the nurse assesses the client to determine if the illness precludes exertion, as with cardiovascular disease [illness involving the heart and blood vessels]. Next, the nurse determines if the client comprehends what is expected. For example, a client recently medicated for post-operative pain may be too lethargic to understand instructions, and to ensure his safety, two nurses are needed to move him in bed. Third, the nurse determines the comfort level of the client. Fourth, the nurse evaluates her knowledge of the procedure and her strength. Last is the determination of whether the client is too heavy or too immobile for the nurse to complete the procedure alone.

Set 3 The following passage is taken from an introductory accounting textbook.[2] It explains what to do if the first attempt to balance the account fails, which means that an error has been made.

When a trial balance does not balance, an error or errors are indicated. To locate the error or errors, check the journalizing, posting, and trial balance preparation steps in their reverse order. First check the addition of the columns in the trial balance to see that no error in addition was made. Then check to see that the account balances were correctly copied from the ledger. Then recalculate the account balances. If at this stage the error or errors have not been found, check the posting and then the original journalizing of the transactions.

Direction Words

In addition to signal words that point out the steps in a set of directions, the reader must be alert to other words that are important to understanding written directions. We will call these direction words. Often direction words will indicate a location. Notice the underlined direction words in the following examples.

The decimal should be moved to the <u>right</u>.

A line must be drawn down the <u>left</u> side of the page.

The screw should be placed <u>over</u> the washer.

It may be helpful to draw a circle around direction words to make them stand out.

Other direction words that appear in written instructions are *precede, preceded by* and *preceding.* You remember that the prefix **pre** means "before" and the combining forms **cede** and **ceed** mean "come." So *precede* means "come before or in front of."

the preceding page	means	the page that comes before
Bob preceded John	means	Bob came first
5 is preceded by 4	means	4 comes first

Other direction words are *consecutive* and *succeeding. Consecutive* means the items come immediately one after another in order and without gaps. *Succeeding* means that which comes after. The preceding pages are the pages that come before this one. The succeeding pages are the pages that come after this one. The next four consecutive pages are pages 89, 90, 91, and 92.

EXERCISE 3

Answer the questions following each sentence.

1. The diagram is on the page preceding page 12.

   What is the page number where the diagram is located? _____

2. The right hand should be placed above and the left hand beneath the line.

   Which hand should be under the line? _____

3. The end of the war was preceded by demonstrations.

   What came first, the end of the war or the demonstrations? _____

   _____

4. The compilation of the list must be succeeded by a final search.

   Which comes last, the list or the search? _____

5. The outbreak of disease preceded the pollution of the water.

   Which came first, the disease or the pollution? _____

6. The number succeeding the letter *J* is 49.

   Which comes first, *J* or 49? _____

7. The most effective solution is the one that preceded Johnson's suggestion.

Did the most effective solution come before or after Johnson's suggestion?

_____

8. The number preceding the letter *A* is 589.

Which comes last, 589 or the letter *A*? _____

9. The blip on the computer screen will succeed the error input message.

Which will come first, the blip or the error input message?_____

10. The number 5 must precede 7, whereas the number 2 must be preceded by 8. The number 1 must be succeeded by 3, and 4 must succeed 6.

Put the numbers in the correct consecutive order according to these

directions. _____

Technical Words in Written Directions

Written directions often contain technical vocabulary words. Frequently these words are defined either directly or by use of punctuation clues. It is important that you note the definitions of such words and mark them. Look at this example.

> The procedure for subtracting whole numbers is as follows. Subtract the digits in the subtrahend, the number you subtract, from the corresponding digits in the minuend, the number from which you subtract. Work from right to left. If any digit in the subtrahend is greater than the corresponding digit [the digit immediately above it] in the minuend, increase the digit in the minuend by 10 by taking 1 from the digit in the next higher place. Check by adding the difference, the answer in subtraction, to the subtrahend. Their sum should equal the minuend.

Many students when faced with a set of directions like this suffer a total breakdown of confidence. Every sentence is loaded with important details and there are no signal words. However, notice that the technical words (subtrahend, minuend, difference) are defined for you. Your first step, then, is to mark the definitions and be sure you understand the technical words. Then break the set of directions into steps and number each step. Note that the word *sum* in math is a technical word. It was introduced and defined earlier in the book from which this passage was taken.

When dealing with a set of directions like the one in the example above, try attacking it by first separating out the technical words.

subtrahend = number you subtract

minuend   = the number from which you subtract

difference   = the answer in subtraction

sum   = the answer in addition

Then rewrite the directions and number the steps.

1. Work from right to left.

2. If the number you subtract is larger than the one right above it, add 10 to the number you subtract from by taking 1 from the number before it.

3. Check by adding the answer to the number you subtracted to see if it equals the number you subtracted from.

This set of directions illustrates just how important it is to understand technical vocabulary. You cannot understand the directions if you do not understand the technical words. In your college textbooks, once a term is introduced and defined, it will continue to be used. The author assumes that if a term is defined for you in Chapter One of the book, you will know what the term means when it is used in Chapter Two.

If you are not clear on a technical word that appears in a set of directions and if the word is not defined for you, look to see if a glossary is included in your book. If not, use the index at the back of the book to look up the word you are unsure of. There will be page numbers listed after the word. On the first page listed or on the page number printed in boldface ink, you will probably find the word's definition. If not, ask your instructor or a classmate for the definition.

Let's try one more set of directions taken from a textbook for a course in critical thinking or reasoning.[3] This passage explains statistical concepts, in particular, measurements of central tendency—a way to tell the average performance of a group. For example, you might want to be able to determine the average test grade made by a class.

Another common measure of central tendency is the **median,** which is simply the middle number when the numbers have been arranged in order. To get the median of the numbers 1, 4, 2, 6, 9, we must first arrange them in order: 1, 2, 4, 6, 9. The middle number, or median, in this group is 4. Whenever there is an even number of items in the group, the median is taken to be the average of the two in the middle. Thus, the median of the numbers 1, 2, 4, 6, 8, 9, is 5.

Using the method we discussed before, we first make sure we understand the technical term.

median = middle number when numbers are in order

There is only one signal word, *first,* and we use that to start the list of steps:

1. Arrange numbers in order.

2. Find middle number; this is the median.

3. If number of items is an even number, median is average of the two middle ones.

EXERCISE 4

For each set of directions do the following:

• Read the entire set of directions first.

• Underline the essential thought.

• Draw a box around signal words.

• Number each step.

• Answer the questions after each set of directions.

Set 1   The following is a set of test directions.

For each statement, write false in the blank if the statement is not true; write true if the statement is not false. Then in the space following statements you think are untrue, write a statement that will make it true.

1. What must you write in the blanks? _____

2. What must you do besides write in the blanks? _____

Set 2   This passage is typical of one that you might find in a book used in a health course.

An emergency technique that every person in the family should know is mouth-to-mouth resuscitation. This rescue breathing technique is used to revive a victim when breathing has stopped. First, the mouth of the victim must be cleared of any objects, vomit, food, or mucus. Then place the person on a firm surface such as the floor or a table. Next tilt the head back with the chin up so that the tongue does not roll back and choke him. Fourth, pinch off his nose. Place your mouth over his and blow gently until you see his chest rise. Next remove your mouth and let his lungs empty as you take a quick breath yourself. Repeat the procedure about twenty times a minute.

1. What is the step preceding placing your mouth over his and blowing?

_____

2. What is the fifth step? _____

3. What is the second step? _____

4. What is the sixth step? _____

5. What step precedes tilting his head back? _____

Set 3   These directions are typical of those in a math book.

To divide by decimals turn the **divisor** (the number by which you are to divide) into a whole number if it is not already one by moving the decimal point the necessary places to the right. Then move the decimal point in the **dividend** (the number to be divided) the same number of places to the right.

1. In what direction do you move the decimal point? _____

2. How many places do you move the decimal point in the dividend?

_____

3. The mathematical symbol ÷ means "divided by." You read the problem 23.45 ÷ 326.15 as "23.45 divided by 326.15." In this problem:

Which number is the divisor? _____

Which number is the dividend? _____

4. Rewrite the problem in the following space with the decimal points moved correctly so that each number becomes a whole number.

_____

Set 4   Study the line of numbers below and then follow the directions that are below it.

8   3   4   7   1   2   9   6   5

1. Draw a circle around the number in the middle if it is even; draw a triangle around it if it is odd.

2. Draw a star beneath the number succeeding 9.

3. Draw a square around each even number preceding an odd number.

4. Draw an X above each odd number preceded by an even number.

5. If the first four consecutive numbers have the same sum as the last four consecutive numbers, draw a star over the center number.

Set 5   This passage is typical of one that you might find in a study skills book in a section on learning technical vocabulary words.

> First decide on the words you want to learn. Write each word on one side of an index card. Then on the other side of the card write the definition of the word as it is given in your text. Next practice by saying the word out loud and then reading the definition out loud. Finally test yourself by reading the word and trying to say the definition without looking at it. Check to see if you said the definition correctly.

List the steps in learning vocabulary words using this method.

1. _____

2. _____

3. _____

4. _____

5. _____

6. _____

Set 6   In doing this set of directions, be sure to follow carefully the instructions given at the beginning of Exercise 4.

1. If the letter *S* is preceded in the alphabet by the letter *N*, draw a square around the word *circle* in step 2 of these directions.

2. If the letters *K* and *L* are in consecutive order in the alphabet, draw a circle in the lower left corner of this page.

3. If Wednesday is succeeded by Friday, draw a triangle in the lower right corner of this page.

4. If you are not a cat, simply write your name at the center bottom of this page and ignore all of the other directions in this set.

Set 7   The following passage is typical of one you might find in a book used in a foundations of business course. It lists the steps to follow in a management technique called management by objectives (MBO). Read the directions below and then in the space provided, list the steps in order.

A widely used management technique used by many companies is called **management by objectives** or **MBO.** This technique is aimed at improving the performance and the overall motivation of workers by having the employees participate in setting their own goals. First the employee discusses his or her job description with the job supervisor. Together they set short-term performance goals and decide on a time period for meeting the goals. The employee then meets regularly with the supervisor to discuss progress in meeting the goals. At the end of the defined period, the supervisor and the employee meet again to evaluate the employee's success in meeting the goals. There is also an evaluation each time the employee and the supervisor meet during the defined time period.

Steps in the MBO technique:

_____

_____

_____

_____

_____

Summary

In order to do well in college, it is essential to be able to read and follow written directions. Imperative sentences in which the subject is understood to be "you, the reader" are most often used in written directions. The core parts that express the essential thought of an imperative sentence are the understood subject, the verb, and the direct object. However, written directions contain other key words that are necessary for understanding exactly what to do.

Written directions will often contain signal words that point out the steps to be done. Not every step will be signalled by such a word, however. Reading written directions calls for active reading. As you read directions you should box signal words, underline key words, and number the steps. Comprehension of written directions will be enhanced or improved by visualizing each step and thinking about the logic in the sequence of the directions. Comprehension can be checked by trying to repeat the directions either orally (saying them) or by writing out the key words in each step.

Direction words are an important aspect of written directions. Direction words may indicate a location, position, or direction. Direction words like *preceding, preceded by, succeeding,* and *consecutive* can be confusing, and the reader should be clear on their meanings.

Written directions may contain many technical words. These words may be defined in the directions, or it may be assumed that the words are known. If the meaning of a technical word is not known, the reader should check the glossary or index for a definition or should ask the instructor or a classmate for help.

Reading written directions requires careful reading. The ability to read directions accurately is a skill essential to success in college.

6 Reading Paragraphs

Many college students are overwhelmed by the amount of information in college textbooks. Because so much of the information is new to them, they have difficulty separating out what is important to learn. Everything looks important.

One of the most important reading skills for college textbook reading is the ability to find the main idea and supporting details in a paragraph. Main ideas and primary details represent the "meat" of a textbook. This is the "important stuff" you are expected to learn.

Just as understanding the structure of sentences can help in sentence comprehension, understanding the structure of a paragraph can help in paragraph comprehension. You may have taken a writing or composition course in which you learned how to write a unified paragraph. The writing skills you learned to use to compose a paragraph can help you understand a paragraph someone else has written.

A paragraph is a group of sentences that are related. What makes the sentences related is that they are all about one topic, and taken together, the sentences express one general idea. Each sentence in the paragraph either expresses that one idea or tells something about the idea. In order to understand the structure of the paragraph, you must first understand clearly the concepts of "general" and "specific."

General and Specific

A term is general if it refers to a group. A term is specific if it refers to one item in that group. The word *plant* refers to a group of things that includes vegetables, fruits, flowers, trees, bushes, and many others. So we could have the following situation as the step diagram shows:

| general | = | plant |

| specific | = | flower |

"Plant" is more general than "flower" because the group named by the term *plant* includes *flower*. The group named by *plant* is larger than the group named by *flower*. Look at it this way:

All flowers are plants.   *but*   Not all plants are flowers.

All flowers are plants.   *but*   All plants are not flowers.

The entire group of flowers is included in the group named by *plants*. But the entire group of plants is not included in the group named by *flowers* because there are plants that are not flowers (trees, for example). The group named by *plant* is larger than the group named by *flowers* because "plant" includes all flowers and more. *Flower* is smaller than *plant* because *flower* does not include all plants. This concept can be shown visually using circles:

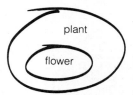

The larger circle labeled "plant" is more general than the smaller circle labeled "flower." The smaller circle labeled "flower" is more specific than the larger circle labeled "plant."

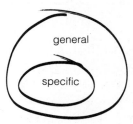

EXERCISE 1

In this exercise you are given two terms. One is general, the other specific. You are to draw two circles, one inside the other. Label the larger circle with the general term. Label the smaller circle with the specific term.

1. science

   biology

2. semester

   academic year

3. vehicle

   bus

4. college

   educational institution

5. occupation

   sales clerk

What may be confusing is that a term that is specific in one situation may be general in another. Given the two terms *flower* and *rose*, which is the general term? *Flower*, of course. But given the two terms *plant* and *flower*, which is the general term? *Plant*. A term is general or specific in relation to another term. The following step diagram illustrates this concept.

General	Plant	Flower
specific	flower	rose

EXERCISE 2

In the following exercise you are given two terms. Fill in the step diagram with the general term first and the specific term below it.

1. building

    store

2. ice cream shop

    store

3. dog

    animal

4. dog

    collie

5. math course

    curriculum

6. Algebra I

    math course

7. food

    fruit

8. apple

    fruit

9. chair

    furniture

10. chair

    rocker

Remember that a term is general or specific in relationship to another term. For example, *flower* is general in relation to *rose*, but *flower* is specific in relation to *plant*. If we arrange those three terms on one step diagram, we would have the following:

```
|plant_____
        |flower_____
            |rose_____
```

This step diagram has three levels ranging from the most general term, *plant*, to the most specific term, *rose*. Study the following illustration of two-level, three-level, and four-level step diagrams. Notice that the first term on the diagram is the most general and the last is the most specific.

```
Two levels        |building_____
                      |store_____

Three levels      |building_____
                      |store_____
                          |ice cream shop_____

Four levels       |building_____
                      |store_____
                          |ice cream shop_____
                              |Martin's ice cream shop
```

Notice that store is one type of building; there are other terms that would fit under *building*, for example, *apartment building*. But if we were to use *apartment building* on the second level, we could not, of course, use *ice cream shop* on the third because ice cream shop is not one kind of apartment building. The terms on the levels are interrelated because each term is more general or more specific in relation to another term.

We could start at the top of the last diagram and say "Building is more general than store; store is more general than ice cream shop; ice cream shop is more general than Martin's ice cream shop."

Or we could start at the bottom of the diagram and say "Martin's ice cream shop is more specific than ice cream shop; ice cream shop is more specific than store; store is more specific than building."

EXERCISE 3

In this exercise you are given three related terms. Arrange them on a step diagram with the most general term on the top step and the most specific term on the bottom step.

1. footwear

    shoe

    sandal

2. kitchen

    house

    room

3. corporation

    automobile manufacturer

    Ford Company

4. news program

    CBS Evening News

    television program

5. raincoat

    outerwear

    coat

6. painting

    art

    water color

7. sports

    javelin throw

    track and field event

8. sentence

   paragraph

   word

9. July

   year

   month

10. political cartoon

   newspaper

   editorial page

EXERCISE 4

In the following exercise, you are given two words and are asked to supply a third word to complete the list. The words should be listed with the most general word first and the most specific word last. The first two are done for you.

1. dessert

   pie _____

   cherry pie

2. types of government _____

   democracy

   United States of America

3. vehicle

   _____

   Oldsmobile

4. institution of higher education

   two-year college

   _____

5. public transportation

airline

_____

6. prose

_____

biography

7. _____

sibling

brother

8. reference book

_____

Webster's *New Collegiate Dictionary*

9. _____

automobile race

Indy 500

10. entertainment

movie

_____

EXERCISE 5

In the blank beside each statement, write **T** if the statement is true and **F** if the statement is false. For a statement to be marked true, the entire statement must be true. If any part of the statement is false, the entire statement must be marked false. This is a technique you can use on any true-false test. If you get stuck on a statement, try drawing a step diagram to help you visualize the relationship of the terms in the statement.

_____ **1.** All flowers are plants.

_____ **2.** Not all plants are flowers.

_____ **3.** All roses are plants.

_____ **4.** All plants are roses.

_____ **5.** Not all roses are plants.

_____ **6.** Not all plants are roses.

_____ **7.** All roses are flowers.

_____ **8.** All plants are flowers.

_____ **9.** All roses are not plants.

_____ **10.** All plants are not flowers.

_____ **11.** Some flowers are roses.

_____ **12.** Some plants are flowers.

_____ **13.** Some plants are not flowers.

_____ **14.** Some roses are not plants.

_____ **15.** Some flowers are not roses.

_____ **16.** Some roses are not flowers.

_____ **17.** Some flowers are not plants.

_____ **18.** *Flower* is a more general term than *plant*.

_____ **19.** *Plant* is a more specific term than *rose*.

_____ **20.** *Rose* is a more specific term than *flower*.

_____ **21.** *Flower* is a more general term than *plant*, and *plant* is a more specific term than *rose*.

_____ **22.** *Plant* is a more specific term than *flower*, and *flower* is a more specific term than *rose*.

_____ **23.** *Flower* is a more general term than *plant*, and *plant* is a more general term than *rose*, and *rose* is a more general term than *flower*.

_____ **24.** *Plant* is a more general term than *flower*, and *flower* is a more general term than *rose*, and *rose* is a more specific term than *flower*.

_____ **25.** *Rose* is a more specific term than *flower*, and *flower* is a more specific term than *plant*, and *plant* is a more general term than *flower*.

Structure of a Paragraph

As we said earlier, a paragraph is a group of sentences about one topic, and each sentence in the paragraph either expresses a general idea about that topic or tells something about the general idea. To help you understand the structure of a paragraph we will now introduce some technical terms.

1. **Topic:** the subject of the paragraph, what is being talked about in the paragraph

2. **Main idea:** the general idea expressed in the paragraph, the point being made about the topic

3. **Primary supporting details:** the specific things being said about the main idea, how the author proves or supports his or her point about the topic

The primary supporting details are sometimes called primary details or major details.

Think about what you do when you compose a paragraph. First you must decide what to write about. This is your topic. Let's say that you are a single parent and are returning to college after having been out of school for a number of years. You decide to write about that. Your topic, then, is "returning to college." Then you must decide what it is you want to say about returning to college. Perhaps you want to express the general idea that your decision to return to college meant that you had to make a lot of changes in your life. Your main idea, then, is "my decision to return to college involved many adjustments." Now you must decide how you are going to prove the point that your returning to college involved many adjustments by thinking of specific adjustments you had to make. You think about having to find transportation, about having to cut down on the number of hours you work, about having to find child care for your children, and about having less money to spend on fun. All these things are your primary supporting details for the main idea that your returning to college involved many adjustments.

Recognizing the topic, main idea, and primary supporting details is essential to comprehending your textbooks fully. To help you find these elements, ask yourself three questions about the paragraph:

1. What is the author talking about? The answer to this question will be the **topic** of the paragraph.

2. What is the point the author is making about the topic? The answer to this question will be the **main idea** of the paragraph.

3. How does the author support or prove the point? The answer to this question will be the **primary supporting details** of the paragraph.

You might remember the three questions more easily if you condense them into a briefer form:

What? = **topic**

Point? = **main idea**

Proof? = **primary supporting details**

Now let's try this technique on a paragraph:

You can improve your concentration by controlling your study environment, the place you have chosen to study. First, choose a study area that is quiet. Then make sure you have adequate work space and good lighting. Finally remove from the area any distractions such as pictures or books that might draw your attention away from your studies.

Topic	What?	Concentration
Main idea	Point?	You can improve your concentration by controlling your study environment.
Primary supporting details	Proof?	1. Choose a quiet area.
		2. Have adequate work space and good lighting.
		3. Remove distractions.

The author of this paragraph told you what her point was in the first sentence. The sentence that expresses the main idea of a paragraph is called the topic sentence. In the topic sentence the author is saying, "Here is what I want to say about the subject I'm writing about in this paragraph. Here is my point, the reason I wrote this paragraph."

EXERCISE 6

Fill in the blank with the correct word.

1. The _____ is the subject of the paragraph or what is being talked about in the paragraph.

2. The _____ is the point the author is making about the topic of the paragraph.

3. The _____ prove or support the main idea.

4. The _____ is the general thought expressed in the paragraph.

5. The _____ are the specific things being said about the main idea.

Locating the Topic Sentence

In a paragraph, the sentence that expresses the point the author wants to make (the main idea) is called the **topic sentence.** Because the topic sentence tells what that point is, locating the topic sentence is one of the most important skills for textbook reading. The primary supporting details support the main idea by telling more about it. Primary details explain specific points about the general idea the author is presenting.

In composition classes students are often told to put their topic sentence first in the paragraph they are writing. This is a good idea because it helps beginning writers focus their attention on the point they are trying to make in the paragraph. Then each sentence written after the first must directly relate to and support the topic sentence, the main idea. Because of this practice, many students have the mistaken idea that the first sentence in *any* paragraph is the topic sentence. Because they know that it is important to mark main ideas in their textbooks, they often underline the first sentence of each paragraph believing that they are marking the "important stuff," the main idea.

However, authors of textbooks are not beginning writers. The first sentence *may* be the topic sentence and often *is* the topic sentence. However, contrary to popular belief, the topic sentence is not always the first sentence in the paragraph. It may be the second sentence, or the middle sentence, or the last sentence. Or there may not be a topic sentence at all. Authors may not come right out and tell you what their point is. They may leave it to you to figure out the main idea on your own. If there is no topic sentence, the main idea is implied (not stated). We will talk more about implied main ideas later. For now let's concentrate on those situations where the main idea is stated in a topic sentence.

Because the topic sentence may be anywhere in the paragraph, including the last sentence, you must read the paragraph all the way through before deciding what the main idea of the paragraph is. Many students find this very hard to do. They know they should be marking the "important stuff," and they know that the main idea is important. The problem often is that in a textbook every sentence seems important when you first read it. You cannot find the sentence that expresses the general idea of the paragraph until you have finished the paragraph and know all it has to say.

Sometimes an author will signal the main idea by using phrases such as "in conclusion" or "in summary." We will call these phrases conclusion signal words. When you come to phrases such as these in a sentence, consider whether that sentence expresses the general thought or the point the author is making in the paragraph. However, remember that reading is a thinking activity. You cannot automatically assume that if you see what looks like a conclusion signal word in a sentence, that sentence expresses the main idea. You must still ask yourself "What is the point the author is making about the topic?" The following phrases are often used to signal a main idea:

in conclusion	to conclude	the point is
it is important	in summary	to sum up
to summarize	thus	therefore
in short	on the whole	consequently
as a result	in other words	it can be seen that

In the following exercise you are asked to decide on the topic and the main idea of each paragraph. Each paragraph has a topic sentence. Remember the questions you should ask yourself:

Topic   = What is the paragraph about?

Main idea = What is the point being made about the topic?

EXERCISE 7

For each of the paragraphs that follow, write the topic in the space provided. Look for conclusion signal words and box any you find. Then locate and underline the topic sentence.

1. Topic: _____

   College differs from high school in several important ways. In the first place, the college student generally does not attend classes in a course every day of the week but rather two or three times a week. Night courses might meet only once a week. In the second place, in college more information is presented in a shorter length of time. For example, a high school English course may be a year-long course whereas a college English course may be only one semester long. Finally, the college student is expected to do most of his learning on his own outside of class; he is expected to be an independent learner.

2. Topic: _____

The course syllabus or course outline students generally receive on the first day of class will usually give the instructor's name and office location. It may also list the topics that will be covered in the course along with the objectives of the course—those things the student will be expected to do at the end of the course. The required textbook and test dates may also be given. The point is that the course syllabus contains much important information and should be read carefully.

3. Topic: _____

One major source of information in a college course is the instructor. Through lecture the instructor will give the student much of the information the student is expected to learn for the course. Of course, the textbook is another major source of information. The student should complete all reading assignments as they are made and not wait until immediately before a test to do the reading. Some students do not realize the importance of class discussion as a major source of information in the college classroom. In a class discussion, the instructor will often elicit (draw out) from students points that are important to learn. A final source of information is the supplemental material that the instructor may make available. Supplemental materials might include handouts, duplicated materials, and books or articles placed on reserve in the library or listed on the course outline as suggested but not required reading. In summary, there are four major sources of information for a college course.

4. Topic: _____

There are several factors that can prevent effective listening in a lecture situation. One factor is physical distractions such as noise outside the classroom. Another factor that prevents the student from getting the important points from the lecture is a lack of preparation by the student. For example, a student who has not done the reading assignment will not be as able to recognize the important points in the lecture. A third factor is the lecturer herself who may speak so rapidly that the student has difficulty following the lecture.

5. Topic: _____

In a lecture situation, the student should select a seating location that will allow him or her to see the lecturer. It is easier to concentrate and to understand what a person is saying if one is able to see the person's face. If possible, the student should select a seat near the middle of the room so that activity outside the classroom will not be a distraction. It is important that the student do everything possible to prepare to listen effectively before a lecture begins. In addition to choosing a favorable seating location, the student should complete any reading assignments before the lecture. If the lecturer speaks rapidly, it may be possible to team up with a classmate. One person could be responsible for information given orally (spoken) while the other is responsible for information delivered in written form on the board, the overhead projector, or by film slides. After class the students could compare notes and fill in any missing information.

6. Topic: _____

To increase comprehension in textbook reading, students should learn to preview the chapter before reading. The first step in previewing is to read the title, which, of course, is the topic of the chapter. You should ask yourself how this chapter fits in with the preceding one. You should also ask yourself what you already know about the topic of this chapter and what you want to find out about the topic. The next step in previewing is to read the section headings to discover the outline of the chapter. The third step in previewing is to note the graphic aids (graphs, pictures, tables) in the chapter. Then you should read the chapter summary if there is one. Finally you should read any questions that appear at the end of the chapter to see what points the author thinks are important. If there are chapter objectives listed at the beginning of the chapter, you should also note these.

7. Topic: _____

Marking the textbook has three benefits for the student. It increases comprehension and concentration. It sets up the textbook for review without having to reread the entire chapter. It enables the student to test herself on the textbook.

8. Topic: _____

In order to prepare to study effectively for a test, the student should first find out what material will be covered on the test. The course outline or the assignment sheet for the course may provide that information. The instructor may also tell students what material will be covered when announcing the test. In addition, the student needs to know when the test will be, of course, so that sufficient study time can be scheduled. The student also needs to know whether the test will be an objective test or an essay test or a combination of the two. Finally the student needs to find out whether there is a time limit for taking the test. In conclusion, before a student can begin to study in an effective manner for a test, certain information about the test itself must be known.

9. Topic: _____

Students learn in different ways. Some students learn best by writing out the information to be learned. Other students need to hear the information and learn best by reciting or saying the information aloud. Still other students learn through a combination of first writing the information and then reciting.

10. Topic: _____

Poor test results can be used to improve future test grades if the test is examined carefully. The student should examine the wrong answers to discover whether those questions test material from the textbook or from lecture notes. If missed questions come mostly from lecture notes, then the student knows that his note-taking technique is not effective. The student should also try to discover whether he missed questions because of poor test-taking techniques such as not following directions or misreading the questions. Then the student should examine the wrong answers to see if the questions are testing details or main ideas. It may be that the student is concentrating on details, for example, when the test was designed to test major concepts or main ideas.

EXERCISE 8

The following passages are typical of what you might find in college textbooks. For each passage, determine the topic and write it in the space provided. Also look for conclusion signal words and box them. Then ask yourself "What is the point the author is making about the topic?" Find the sentence that expresses that point—the main idea—and underline it. Be sure to read the introduction describing the type of textbook in which the passage might be found or from which the passage was extracted. In some passages taken from textbooks you will find material in brackets [ ] that has been added to the original passage in order to clarify it for you.

1. This passage is typical of one you might find in a book used in a "Marriage and the Family" course.

Topic: _____

A divorce often results in financial difficulties. Child care may also become a problem both in terms of paying for it and in terms of feeling overwhelmed with having the sole responsibility of caring for the children. Even in the most friendly of divorces there is an emotional toll akin to that which results from the death of a spouse. Thus divorce may mean that many financial and emotional adjustments must be made. Many divorced people list loneliness as the number one problem.

2. This passage is typical of one you might find in a book used in a foundations of business, business management, or business finance course.

Topic: _____

In the early 1950s, banks (and later large chain stores such as Sears) began issuing charge cards as a way of providing credit to their customers and offered revolving or installment payment plans that allowed customers to pay a minimum on their balance with the remainder deferred—with a finance charge on the unpaid balance, of course. On the other hand, travel and entertainment cards were not meant to provide credit because the cardholders were required to pay their bills in full at the end of each month. This type of card was meant as a convenience for the cardholder who would not need to carry large amounts of cash but could charge costs made at participating establishments and companies. Thus, customers were provided with two new ways of charging purchases.

3. This passage is taken from a composition book, in a chapter entitled "Paragraphs: Units of Development."[1]

Topic: _____

Paragraphs serve several purposes for you and your readers. You can use them to divide your subject into manageable units of information. By grouping ideas into paragraphs, you show the relationship of ideas to one another and their significance to your overall purpose. You can also use paragraphs to control emphasis. By placing a paragraph in a particular position, you demonstrate the relative importance of an idea in your essay. Finally, you can use paragraphs to establish rhythm. By interrupting a series of long paragraphs with a short paragraph, or by creating a series of brief paragraphs, you establish and vary cadence in your writing.

4. This passage is typical of one that might appear in a textbook used in a reading, English, or philosophy course, from a section discussing the meanings of words.

Topic: _____

Some words have both denotation and connotation. The denotation of a word is what might be called the "dictionary meaning" or the thing that the word names. For example, the denotation of the word *slob* might be "a person who is untidy." The connotation of a word is the "emotional baggage" that a word might carry or the feelings that a word might arouse in a person. For example, the word *slob* may arouse a feeling of disapproval. The point is that the reader should be aware of the connotation of a word as well as its denotation.

5. This passage is typical of one you might find in a book for a course in foundations of business, business management, or data processing.

Topic: _____

In a management information system, *scheduled listings* are the most common type of report. These are reports that are generated from regularly processed files such as inventory records or payroll accounts and are sent to those persons who need them. A *demand report* is produced at the request of the person who wishes to receive it and contains only the information requested. A list of customers who have not paid their bills is an example of an *exception report*, which alerts the manager to some situation out of the ordinary. Finally, in order to make plans for the future, *predictive reports* are produced that forecast the future behavior of the economy and the company based on past performance. In conclusion, there are four different types of reports that a management information system can produce.

6. This paragraph is taken from a psychology textbook; it explains different theories of memory.[2]

Topic: _____

According to [Atkinson and Shiffrin's storage and transfer model] explanation for the way memory works, all of us have three different types of memory. First, material comes through our senses—our eyes, ears, our nose, and so forth—into **sensory memory (SM).** In less than a second, this information either disappears or is transferred from sensory memory into **short-term memory (STM),** where it may stay for up to 20 seconds. If it does not disappear at this stage, it moves into **long-term memory (LTM),** where it may remain for the rest of our life.

7. This passage is taken from a book about writing that might be used in a composition or writing class.[3]

Topic: _____

The most common form of communication is talking, but writing is different from talking. When you talk, you almost always have an audience who will respond to you. Likewise, you can respond to them. They can ask you questions when they don't understand, they can look puzzled, or they can rephrase what you have said, repeating it back to you in their own words to make sure they understand. You, in turn, can back up to provide information you forgot, can pick up where you left off after an interruption, and can use facial expressions, body movements, and voice changes to help express your meaning. When you write, however, you don't have the advantage of this give and take with your readers. They must be able to understand clearly your ideas and feelings only from your printed words.

8. This passage is taken from a book that might be used in a psychology course.[4]

Topic: _____

When placed in similar situations, each of us has different feelings. Some of us become emotionally charged at an important football game, while others find football a bore. While most people become deeply saddened at the loss of a loved one, some people seem to be cold and to lack feelings. Almost everyone would agree that crying is a strong emotional reaction; but people cry when they are happy *and* when they are sad. A woman may cry at the birth of her child *and* at the loss of a close friend. When researchers first began to study emotional behavior like crying, they realized that there was a wide range of emotions that needed to be evaluated: love, joy, fear, disgust, anger. These emotions had motivating properties because they would impel and direct a person's behavior toward actions. Feelings of dependency might direct a person's behavior toward seeking help. Anger might cause feelings of hostility or revenge. Emotion is, therefore, directly involved in motivation.

9. This passage is taken from a book that might be used in a writing or composition course when learning how to write a research paper.[5]

Topic: _____

Students are often puzzled about how much of the [research] paper should consist of their original writing, and how much of material drawn from researched sources. No exact rule exists. You should not write a paper consisting of a string of quotations and paraphrases but containing nothing of your own. Nor should you glut the paper entirely with your own notions, with only a token quotation or paraphrase added here and there to give the illusion of research. Ideally, the paper should consist of information from sources blended judiciously with your own commentary and interpretation. Certainly you should say what you think, but you should also say why you think it—what evidence exists to support your opinions; which authorities on the subject agree with you; and why those of a different opinion are probably in error. In sum, the paper demands not merely opinionated conclusions, but conclusions supported by other opinions.

10. This passage is taken from a textbook that might be used in a biology course.[6]

    Topic: _____

    This theory [Charles Darwin's theory of evolution] consists of two major parts: the concept of evolutionary change and the concept of natural selection. First, Darwin rejected the notion that living creatures are the immutable [unchangeable] products of a sudden creation, that they exist now in precisely the form in which they have always existed. He maintained that, on the contrary, change is the rule, that the organisms living today have descended by gradual change from ancient ancestors quite unlike themselves. Second, Darwin declared that it is *natural selection* that determines the course of the change, and that this guiding factor can be understood in completely mechanistic terms, without reference to conscious purpose or design.

Finding Primary Supporting Details

You will find that a good deal of any test you take in college will ask you to recall details. For example, it will not be enough to know that there are different types of retail businesses; you will need to know what the different types are. It seems clear, then, that being able to find primary supporting details is an essential skill for reading college textbooks. Remember that primary details will directly support the main idea. For example, if the main idea is that there are several advantages of a particular type of retail business, the details will list those advantages. Or if the main idea is that one type of retail business is different from another type, the details will tell *how* they are different. Or if the main idea is a method for starting a retail business, the details will list the steps in that method.

Let's look again at the paragraph on concentration we discussed before but with one sentence added.

Good concentration will make your study time more effective. You can improve your concentration by controlling your study environment, the place you have chosen to study. First, choose a study area that is quiet. Then, make sure you have adequate work space and good lighting. Finally, remove from the area any distractions such as pictures or books that might draw your attention away from your studies.

In this paragraph the first sentence is too broad or general to be the topic sentence. The point the author is making is not that good concentration will make studying more effective, but *how to improve* concentration by controlling the study environment. Why did the author write this paragraph? Not to tell us how concentration will make studying more effective but to tell us how to improve concentration by controlling the study environment. How do you know this is why she wrote the paragraph? Because each detail is a *way to improve* concentration by controlling the study environment. The first sentence is used to introduce the topic of concentration. Notice also that the author uses signal words to point out the details:

First, choose a study area that is quiet.

Then, make sure you have adequate work space and good lighting.

Finally, remove from the area any distractions.

Other signal words that are sometimes used to point out details are the following:

next	others include	last
other	another	also
in addition	additionally	besides
moreover	further	furthermore
equally important	likewise	lastly

When signal words are used, it is sometimes easier to find the details first and then decide what point the details prove, that is, what the main idea is. Let's try it that way on the following paragraph. Watch for signal words and draw a box around any you find.

A mnemonic device is a word or sentence used to help in remembering details. For example, if you want to remember the names of the Great Lakes you might use the word *homes*. This word is made up of the first letter of each of the Great Lakes: *H*uron, *O*ntario, *M*ichigan, *E*rie, *S*uperior. However, there are disadvantages in using mnemonic devices that you should be aware of. In the first place, you must spend some time making up the word or sentence. Then you must remember two things, the device itself and the details the device represents. Further, if you cannot recall one letter in the mnemonic word or sentence, you may not be able to recall the remaining details because you have not really learned them and are depending on rote memorization. Finally, mnemonic devices are best used to recall details and facts, not concepts, principles, or ideas.

First, what is the paragraph talking about? Mnemonic devices. So mnemonic devices is the topic of the paragraph. Next, what signal words help you find the primary supporting details?

In the first place	Further
Then	Finally

Now ask yourself what all of these details prove. Well, they are all *disadvantages of using mnemonic devices*. So is there a sentence in the paragraph that states something about mnemonic devices (the topic) and disadvantages of using mnemonic devices (the primary supporting details)? What about the fourth sentence?

However, there are *disadvantages of using mnemonic devices* that you should be aware of.

The reason the author wrote this paragraph seems to be to point out the disadvantages of using mnemonic devices. The fourth sentence, then, is the topic sentence that states the main idea.

So what about the first three sentences? What are they? They introduce the subject of mnemonic devices, define the term, and give an example of a mnemonic device. They are **secondary details,** sometimes called **minor details,** and are added as explanation or examples to make the paragraph easier to understand. Our concern now, however, is primary details. Primary details directly support the main idea and are used to prove the point the main idea expresses. Look at the following outline to see the relationship of topic, main idea, primary supporting detail, and secondary detail:

Topic	Apples
Main Idea	Apples come in different colors.
Primary Detail	Apples may be red, yellow, or green.
Secondary Detail	Granny Smith apples are green.

Notice that the topic is the most general term and the secondary detail is the most specific. Secondary details, then, are more specific than primary details. Because the main idea is more general than primary and secondary details, the main idea is a statement general enough to include the primary and secondary details.

In your textbooks secondary details will often be examples provided to make a primary detail clearer. Examples may be signalled by the following words:

for instance   such as

for example   illustrated by

Let's analyze the following paragraph:

There are two important considerations in choosing a good brand name for a new product. First it must be easy to remember. Short crisp names like Bic, Wisk, and Sprite are good examples. Second, it must create the right image in the mind of the buyer. For instance, car names such as Chrysler's Le Baron and Ford's Crown Victoria suggest aristocracy and wealth.

Note that the two primary details are signalled by the words *first* and *second* while the secondary details are signalled by the words *examples* and *for instance*.

Topic	What?	Brand names
Main idea	Point?	There are two important considerations when choosing a good brand name.
Primary detail	Proof?	1. Easy to remember
Secondary detail	Example?	a. Bic, Wisk, Sprite
Primary detail	Proof?	2. Create right image
Secondary detail	Example?	a. Le Baron, Crown Victoria

Words like *for example* and *for instance* are sometimes used to signal primary rather than secondary details as in the following example.

Clever marketing can extend the life of a product. For instance, advertising new uses for the product will keep it on the shelves. Another way to extend the product's life is to add new customers by introducing the product into other countries. A further example is to change the way the product is packaged so that it is more attractive.

Topic	Clever marketing
Main idea	Clever marketing can extend the life of a product.

Primary supporting details	
	1. Advertising new uses for the product will keep it on the shelves.
	2. Add new customers by introducing the product into other countries.
	3. Change the way the product is packaged so that it is more attractive.

Here the signal words *for instance* and *example* point out primary details. The main idea is that clever marketing can extend the life of a product. The three primary details prove the point of the main idea by telling *how* clever marketing can extend the life of the product. Remember that secondary details in your texts are often illustrations or examples, that is, a particular case or instance. In the paragraph above, the primary detail "advertising new uses" could be illustrated by the example or particular case of using baking soda to keep the refrigerator fresh.

Some students feel frustrated that they cannot count on a signal word like *for example* to always point out a secondary detail. Such students would like for the reading process to be "cut-and-dried" with the rules clearly spelled out and no room for mistakes. They would like to be certain that whenever they see the signal word *for example* they automatically know that a secondary detail has been signalled. If you see a signal word like "for example," what it is pointing out is most likely a detail. Figuring out whether it is a secondary or primary detail is part of the thinking process that you as an active reader are expected to do.

Because our emphasis is on the skills essential for reading college texts, it is important as you do the next exercise to remember that you will not be reading just one isolated paragraph at a time in your textbook. That paragraph will be in the context of a section of a chapter. Each section of the chapter will give you information that will help you understand the next section. Therefore, you may find locating the primary details in the following paragraphs a little difficult because you have to read the paragraph all by itself without having the advantage of the information in the previous paragraphs. To help you overcome that difficulty, the introduction to each paragraph tells what sort of book the paragraph is taken from or might be found in and tells what that paragraph is about (the topic). Again additional information has been placed in brackets [ ] to help clarify the passage for you. Be sure to read the introduction for each paragraph to understand more clearly what the paragraph is about before you start to search for the primary details.

EXERCISE 9

In this exercise you are to list the primary details in each paragraph. When you list the primary details you need not write out the entire sentence; just write the key words of the sentences that express the details.

For the first five paragraphs, you will be shown by lettered blanks how many primary details to list. The last five paragraphs do not indicate how many details to list.

For each of the following paragraphs:

• Read the introduction and the paragraph through.

• Then go back and draw a box around words that signal primary details.

• List the details in the space provided.

• Draw a line under the topic sentence.

The first one is done for you.

1. This paragraph is taken from a law book for people who are not lawyers or studying to be lawyers. The section this paragraph is taken from discusses law suits.[7]

Litigation is wasteful for several reasons. First court calendars in almost all parts of the country are long and crowded; more legal actions are being brought than there are judges to handle them. Second, litigation involves many appearances in court by your lawyer that are purely routine, but that take him out of his office for at least an hour, depending on how near his office is to the courthouse. Third, no matter how skilled your lawyer is in the area of your lawsuit, he or someone he employs is going to have to do some research to make sure he knows the latest developments in the law on that subject. Fourth, your lawyer will probably have to spend some time checking on the facts you present to him and talking to other people who may be involved in the case.

Primary Supporting Details

a. court calendars are long and crowded

b. litigation involves many court appearances by your lawyer

c. __lawyer must do research__

d. __lawyer must spend time checking facts and talking to people involved in the__

__case__

2. This passage is taken from a psychology textbook from a section entitled "Job Satisfaction." In the parentheses are the names of the people who did the research and the year that the research was published.[8]

The level of satisfaction [with their jobs] is lower, on the average, among young, newly hired workers than among long-term workers (Bass & Ryterband, 1979). One explanation is that older workers have better, higher-paying jobs that offer greater responsibility and challenge. Another is that today's young people, who are better educated than older generations, are harder to satisfy. Neither of the explanations is fully adequate, however (Janson & Martin, 1982). Another possibility is that many young workers start in the wrong jobs and find more suitable ones later on. Still another is that many young people have not yet adjusted to the idea of working 40 or more hours a week and would be dissatisfied in *any* job.

Primary Supporting Details

a. _____

b. _____

c. _____

d. _____

3. This passage comes from a composition textbook in a chapter entitled "The Requirements of Topical Paragraphs."[9]

An effective topical paragraph must meet four requirements. First, it must discuss one topic only; that is, its statements and illustrations must display a *unity* of subject matter, often expressed in a topic sentence.

Second, it must say all that your readers need to know about the topic; it must be *complete* enough to do what it is intended to do. Third, the sentences within the paragraph must exhibit an *order* that your readers can recognize and follow. Fourth, the sentences within the paragraph must display *coherence*, allowing readers to move easily from one sentence to the next without feeling that there are gaps in the sequence of ideas or points.

Primary Supporting Details

a. _____

b. _____

c. _____

d. _____

4. This passage is taken from a composition textbook, from a section discussing prewriting activities.[10]

Because one of the most terrifying moments in this process is starting to write on that blank paper, many writers find it useful to *freewrite* for awhile, just writing with abandon about anything that comes into their heads while they are thinking about a topic. Freewriting is like doing stretching exercises to warm up before jogging: It gets the writing "muscles" relaxed, interested, and ready to go. Freewriting is one of several kinds of prewriting or introductory activities that a writer can do to feel organized about the work and to get started in some direction. Also, it provides an opportunity to get in the mood for writing on a particular topic. Relaxing before starting to work is an important step in developing your concentration. By freewriting you can begin to eliminate distracting noises, sights, or problems that can keep you from starting to write.

Primary Supporting Details

a. _____

b. _____

c. _____

d. _____

e. _____

5. This passage from a sociology book is taken from a section entitled "The One-Parent Family."[11]

A major problem faced by female-headed families is lack of income. In the United States in 1980 the median income for female-headed households was $10,408, while the median income for married couples was $21,023. In Canada, the average income of female-headed families in 1981 was $14,212, while for married couples it was $28,521. A major reason for the income differential is that in female-headed families there can be only one earner, while the majority of married couple households have two earners. But even when compared with families in which only the man works, the average female-headed family suffers from a lower income. A second reason for lower incomes in female-headed families is that nearly two-thirds of women heading such families do not work at full-time jobs. Yet even when a woman is employed full time, her family has a median income two-thirds as much as that of male-headed families in which the wives do not work. A third reason for the lower income of female-headed families (and also for their low rate of employment) is that women who head families are likely to have less education than the average woman. Thus, for example, while only about 16 percent of American women ages 35 to 44 have not graduated from high school, more than 40 percent of the women who head families did not complete high school (much of this lack of education can be attributed to becoming a mother at a young age). The fact that blacks have lower incomes than whites also helps explain the lower income of female-headed American families, since such families are disproportionately black. Finally, of course, women remain less likely to hold high-paying jobs than men do; thus sex bias depresses the incomes of families lacking a male wage earner.

Primary Supporting Details

a. _____

b. _____

c. _____

d. _____

e. _____

6. This paragraph from a business textbook is taken from a section discussing the chief task of a manager—making decisions—and the importance of establishing a system for gathering information.[12]

But the use of secondary data [previously published information] is subject to a number of important limitations. First, the data may be obsolete. The data provided by the 1980 Census of Population is already obsolete in many areas due to the substantial population shifts since 1980. Second, the classification of secondary data may not be usable for the firm. Because the secondary data were originally collected for a specific purpose, they may not be in an appropriate form for a particular decision maker. For example, a retail merchant who is deciding whether to open a new store in a shopping mall may require data on household income for a five-mile area, but the only available data may be collected on a county basis. In still other cases, available data may be of doubtful accuracy. Errors in collecting, analyzing and interpreting the original data may make the information inaccurate. Even the accuracy of the

1980 Census has been questioned on the grounds that information was not obtained from all members of the population. In all such instances, a firm may be forced to collect primary data.

Primary Supporting Details

_____

_____

_____

_____

_____

7. This paragraph taken from a psychology book is from a section discussing drug abuse.[13]

Although heroin addiction seems to receive more attention in the media, this country's most serious drug problem is alcoholism. Somewhere between 8 and 12 million Americans are alcoholics. According to one recent estimate, 1.3 million teenagers and preteenagers have a serious drinking problem. Fifty percent or more of the deaths in automobile accidents each year can be traced to alcohol; in half of all murders either the killer or the victim had been drinking; and some 13,000 people die of liver damage caused by alcohol every year. In addition, the cost in human suffering to the alcoholic and his or her family is impossible to measure.

Primary Supporting Details

_____

_____

_____

_____

_____

8. This paragraph from a book on management is from a section discussing specialization of labor.[14] Specialization of labor is defined as "the division of a complex job into simpler tasks so that one person or group may carry out only identical or related activities."

Despite the advantages of the specialization of labor, its application may not always be desirable. In some organizations, certain jobs have become oversimplified. Too much specialization in the design of jobs may create boredom and fatigue among employees. For example, some people find it very difficult to perform an assembly-line job requiring the tightening of a bolt 1,000 times a day. Typically the higher degree of specialization is found in assembly-line work. Boredom on assembly lines sometimes causes employee turn-over, absenteeism, and a deteriorating quality of output. These negative consequences of specialization may offset its advantages and increase costs.

Primary Supporting Details

_____

_____

_____

_____

_____

9. This paragraph from an introductory sociology book is from a section that discusses studies of infants in institutions, such as orphanages.[15]

As these studies show, human infants need more than just food and shelter if they are to grow and develop normally. Every human infant needs frequent contact with others who demonstrate affection, who respond to attempts to interact, and who themselves initiate interactions with the child. Infants also need contact with people who find ways to interest the child in his or her surroundings and who teach the child the physical and social skills and knowledge that are needed to function. In addition, in order to develop normally, children need to be taught the culture of their society—to be socialized into the world of social relations and symbols that are the foundation of the human experience.

Primary Supporting Details

_____

_____

_____

_____

_____

10. This paragraph is taken from a marketing book, from a section on marketing strategies and different types of marketing categories.[16]

Many firms are already catering to senior citizens and more will be serving this market. For example, some companies have developed housing and "life care" centers designed to appeal to older people. Casio makes a calculator with large, easy-to-read numbers. Publix Super Markets, a big Florida chain, trains employees to cater to older customers. Check-out clerks, for example, give older customers two light bags instead of one heavier one. Some travel agents are finding that senior citizens are an eager market for inexpensive tours and cruises. Other companies offer diet supplements and drug products—often in special easy-to-open packages. And senior citizen discounts at drug stores are more than just a courtesy—the elderly are the biggest market for medicines.

Primary Supporting Details

_____

_____

_____

_____

_____

Locating Implied Main Ideas

Sometimes the author will not write a topic sentence for each paragraph. If there is no topic sentence, does that mean there is no main idea? No. Remember that the main idea of the paragraph is a general thought to which all sentences in the paragraph relate. The main idea is the point the author is making about the topic. If the point is very important or one that is new or different, be assured the author will most likely take no chances and will express that point in a topic sentence. Sometimes the author will think that the main idea is fairly obvious and leave it to you to figure out what the point is. In other words, the main idea will be implied but not explicitly or directly stated. In still other cases, the main idea is expressed in one paragraph, usually at the very end of the paragraph, and the primary details will be in the next paragraph—which will not repeat the main idea. Sometimes the heading of a section will state the main idea and each paragraph in the section will be a set of primary details that support the main idea stated by the heading.

Some students think it is unfair of the author to make the reader figure out what the point is. They have the attitude that if the author wants them to know the point, the author should tell them. This is not the attitude of an active reader. Keep in mind that being active in the reading process will improve your comprehension. An active reader is one who is involved with the text, not simply reading it in a passive way. The active reader reads with a questioning attitude and engages in a silent conversation with the author. One question uppermost in the mind of the active reader is "What is the point being made here?"

Even if the main idea is not expressed in a topic sentence, you can figure out what the author's point is. How? By looking at the details and asking what point the details support or prove. You can infer the main idea from the details.

Actually you make this sort of inference every day. An inference is a statement about the unknown based on the known. For instance, let's say that you are sitting in a classroom that has no windows and you have no idea what the weather is like outside. In other words the weather outside is unknown. You look up as a classmate comes in the door. He is soaking wet, wearing a raincoat, and carrying an umbrella. You remember that the weather report for today said there was a 95 percent chance of rain. You consider the details you know:

- classmate is soaking wet and wearing rain gear

- weather report indicated high probability of rain today

From the details that are known you can make an inference or educated guess about what you do not know: It is raining outside.

You might be thinking that it was pretty obvious that it was raining outside given the details of the weather report and a wet classmate in rain gear. It may be that the reason some students have problems inferring implied main ideas is that they are concerned that their guess is too obvious. Let's analyze the following paragraph.

One type of retail business is the specialty store that offers a narrow range of products, such as a camera store. Another type is the department store that has a variety of products such as clothing, small appliances, jewelry, and luggage. A third type of retail business is the convenience store that offers a variety of products but a limited selection of each product. For example, 7-Eleven stores may offer groceries as well as toiletries, such as toothpaste and shampoo, but will have only a few brands of each.

Topic	Retail businesses
Primary supporting details	1. One type of retail business is the specialty store.
	2. Another type is the department store.
	3. A third type is the convenience store.

What can you infer from the three details? There are three different types of retail businesses. Does that seem too obvious? Well, perhaps that is why the author did not feel the need to express the main idea in a topic sentence. Let's try one more example.

When telling a story, a writer may choose to write about the events in the order that they actually happened, or in a straight chronological order. The use of flashbacks, however, is also effective. Flashbacks interrupt the forward flow of the story to take the reader backward to an earlier time.

Topic	Telling a story
Primary supporting details	1. A writer can use straight chronological order.
	2. The use of flashbacks is effective.
Implied main idea	There are two ways a writer can tell a story.

In the following example from a psychology book, you would have to know what the main idea of the first paragraph is in order to figure out the implied main idea of the second paragraph. This example is included to remind you that the context of a paragraph is the section that the paragraph is in. Sometimes you must use the context of the paragraph (the section it is in) to figure out the implied main idea of the paragraph. In this section the author is discussing the problem of children who continue to wet the bed long after the usual age of toilet training.

> In the past, parents might take such a child to a psychologist, who would put the child on a couch, talk to him (it was usually a "him"), and after a couple of years announce, "Johnny feels great hostility toward his parents. He really wants to urinate on his parents, but he doesn't dare to. So he wets the bed." Such therapy seldom proved effective.
>
> We now know that most bedwetters have small bladders and thus have difficulty getting through the night without urinating. We also know that they are usually deep sleepers and thus do not wake up when they wet the bed.[17]

The main idea of the first paragraph is the last sentence: "Such therapy seldom proved effective." The main idea of the second paragraph is implied: There are two reasons such therapy proved ineffective.

When you are reading, keep asking yourself questions. What is the point the author wants to make? What is the important thing I need to know? Why is the author telling me these details? What is the author trying to prove or illustrate by telling me these details?

EXERCISE 10

For the following paragraphs:

- Draw a box around any signal words that point out details.
- Underline the primary details.
- Write the main idea of the paragraph in the space provided.

Remember that the main idea will be a statement general enough to include the more specific primary details. The first one is done for you.

1. The following passage might be found in a textbook for an introductory business course.

    The <u>convenience store offers</u> a <u>limited selection of brands</u>. The 7-Eleven store, for example, will have only a few brands available. If you have a favorite brand of shampoo, you might not be able to purchase it at a convenience store. [Another] <u>disadvantage</u> of shopping at <u>convenience stores</u> is <u>the price</u> of the <u>products</u> offered. Because the selection is limited the price of the items tends to be more expensive.

Implied main idea: <u>There are two disadvantages of shopping at convenience</u>

<u>stores.</u>

2. The following passage might be found in a textbook for an introductory business course.

   The name "convenience store" is a good description of such businesses because they tend to be located at convenient places. They also offer quick check-out service so that you don't spend a lot of time waiting in line. Another advantage is that they are open long hours, often twenty-four hours a day, so that you can make purchases there when other retail businesses are closed. If you discover at midnight that you need milk for breakfast, the convenience store is the place you are most likely to go.

   Implied main idea: _____

   _____

3. The following passage might be found in a textbook for an introductory business course.

   If you are interested in starting a retail business, you must first decide on the type of business you want. Then you must select a location. This is probably the most important decision you will face because location can make the difference between success and failure. Once that decision is made, you can establish what products or services you will offer. Finally you must decide on a promotional strategy. You must let your potential customers know where you are and what you offer.

   Implied main idea: _____

   _____

4. The following passage might be found in a textbook for a marketing or advertising course.

   Some ads contain information about the product such as automobile advertisements that list the specifications of a certain car. Other advertisements are aimed at creating a good image for the product or business.

McDonald's ads often do not contain information about the product but are designed to make the consumer have a positive feeling about the company. Getting consumers to switch from one brand to another is the purpose of comparative advertising. The taste test ads of Pepsi are an example of such advertisements.

Implied main idea: _____

_____

5. The following passage might be found in a textbook used in a marketing or advertising course.

One way to get information when planning a new product is to conduct a telephone survey. The advantages of such a survey are that the results are known immediately and the cost is relatively inexpensive. However, the results of a telephone survey may not be representative because people without telephones or with unlisted numbers will not be included.

Implied main idea: _____

_____

6. This passage is typical of one you might find in a book for a course in how to gather data (information) from a large number of people by using a sample (a portion of the population).

One way to choose a sample is to use a random sample in which the members of the population are chosen at random. To ensure that the sample is representative, the random sample might need to be quite large. Another method of sampling is to use a stratified sample in which all important groups of the population are represented in the proportion that they actually exist in the population. The members within each group are chosen at random.

Implied main idea: _____

_____

7. This passage is typical of one you might find in a book for an introductory course in business, business finance, business management, or accounting.

Employees may be paid based on the amount of output produced by the worker. A salesperson, for example, might be paid a commission based on the number of sales she makes. Time wages are based on the amount of time spent on a job. Assembly-line workers are typically paid on a per hour basis. Some employee programs include incentive compensation or a bonus to reward employees for outstanding performance. A company might have a profit-sharing plan where a percentage of company profits is distributed to employees.

Implied main idea: _____

_____

8. This paragraph is typical of one that might appear in a book on study skills in a section explaining how to take good classroom notes.

Most students know that it is important to include in their classroom notes anything the instructor writes on the blackboard or on the overhead projector. The instructor might also give verbal clues such as saying "Now this is an important point." Another clue to important information is when the instructor pauses. She is not pausing because she has forgotten what she wanted to say next but to give alert students the opportunity to write down the information she has just given. Body language can also clue in the student to important information. If the instructor wants to make an important point, she will often move toward the students or emphasize the point with her hands. A change in the pace of the lecture is another clue that what is being said is important. Most speakers slow down to emphasize the importance of a point they are making. Finally, a change in the volume of the voice can be a clue. Many speakers know one way to catch the attention of the audience is to speak more softly. However, others will emphasize the importance of what they are saying by speaking more loudly. Either way, the change in the volume of the voice is a way to emphasize what is being said.

Implied main idea: _____

_____

9. The following passage is taken from a psychology text from a section discussing anorexia nervosa, "a condition in which a person refuses to eat adequately and steadily loses weight."[18]

Anorexia nervosa occurs in about one-half of 1 percent of white teenage girls. It is very rare in boys, in black girls, in preteens, and in women past their early 20s. (Although the problem seldom begins later than the early 20s, it may persist through the 20s and beyond.) Anorexia nervosa is generally more severe if it appears in the late teens than if it appears earlier (Halmi, Casper, Eckert, Goldberg, & Davis, 1979). Like other psychological conditions, anorexia nervosa comes in all degrees. Of those who are seriously enough afflicted to consult a physician, about 5 to 10 percent die of starvation.

Implied main idea: _____

_____

10. The following passage is taken from a psychology book from a section entitled "Special Uses of Hypnosis: Surgery and Pain."[19]

A number of studies have reported cases in which individuals undergo surgical incisions and removal of tumors without drugs. These subjects are hypnotized and told that surgery will not be painful. Some studies tell of patients who are able to tolerate surgery without drugs; however, many of the studies have not been conducted with adequate experimental rigor. In addition, the effectiveness of hypnotism in reducing surgical pain has been exaggerated. In many cases in which hypnotism is used, analgesic drugs (pain relievers) are used along with hypnotism. Furthermore, most patients commonly show signs of pain even when they are hypnotized. The skin is particularly sensitive to the surgeon's scalpel, so consequently many hypnotized individuals have some kind of local anesthetic to dull the skin for the initial surgical incision (Barber, Spanos, & Chaves, 1974).

Implied main idea: _____

_____

Summary

There are three essential questions for reading comprehension in regard to college textbooks. The first question is "What is the author talking about?" The answer to this question is the **topic.** Each chapter has a title that gives the topic of the chapter. Most chapters are divided into sections, and each section has a heading in bold print. The heading of the section of the chapter acts as a title for that section and gives the topic of the section.

The second essential question for reading comprehension is "What is the point the author is making about the topic?" The answer to this question is the **main idea.** The main idea of the entire chapter usually is given in the introduction to the chapter. In addition, many textbook chapters include at the beginning of the chapter a list of objectives that serves as an outline of the main ideas for the chapter.

The third essential question for reading comprehension is "What is the evidence the author gives to support the point? How does the author explain or prove the point?" The answer to this question is the **primary supporting details.**

The main idea is often stated, and the sentence that expresses the main idea is called the **topic sentence.** The topic sentence is often the first sentence of the paragraph. However, the topic sentence may be placed anywhere in the paragraph. Sometimes the main idea is expressed in the first sentence of the paragraph and repeated in the last sentence.

If there is no topic sentence, the main idea is said to be **implied.** To find the implied main idea, the primary details are located first. Then the question "What do these details prove?" or "What is the point the author is trying to make by telling me these things?" is asked. The answer to this question is the implied main idea.

The author will often include examples or other information to make the primary details and main ideas clearer. These are the **secondary supporting details.**

Reading comprehension is greatly improved if the reader adopts a questioning attitude. The reader who reads to find the answer to questions is an active reader; the active reader engages in a silent conversation with the author by asking the three essential questions for reading comprehension and then reading to find the answers to those questions.

7 Recognizing Patterns of Organization

Locating the topic, main idea, and primary details are clearly essential to comprehending your college textbooks. This is the important information that you must learn. However, textbook authors do not simply write down the important information as it occurs to them: They arrange the information in some way. For example, it may be that what is important for you to know are the steps in tracing a problem in a computer program. It would make no sense to list those steps in just any old way. Obviously it makes sense to list the steps in the order that they are to be done. The way the information in a textbook is arranged is the **pattern of organization.**

The pattern of organization is determined by what is important about the information the author is giving you. Because what is important about tracing a problem in a computer program is *how to do it*, the pattern of organization must be one that will make the **sequence** of steps clear. To take another example, if what is important about the information the author is giving you about retail businesses is *how they are different*, the author will **contrast** them for you.

Most of the information in college textbooks is arranged in four common patterns: **sequence, listing, compare and contrast, cause and effect.** In this chapter you learn how recognizing the pattern of organization of the information in a textbook chapter can help you decide what is important to learn about the information.

Sequence Pattern of Organization

A **sequence** is a set of details put into a particular order. What is important to learn about the information is the order. A set of directions is, of course, a sequence of steps to follow. Obviously, what is important to learn about directions is the order in which one is to do the steps in the directions. Because reading written directions is such an important skill in college textbook reading, a whole chapter—Chapter 5—of this book is devoted to it.

Being able to recognize a sequence pattern of organization is important in college reading. For example, in science courses that have a lab requirement, you will have to be able to follow a procedure for a lab experiment. If you do not do the steps in the experiment in the proper order, you might have a disaster on your hands. The same thing is true of data processing and computer programming courses. Math and science courses require that you comprehend numerical order whereas a course such as astronomy requires that you understand spatial location, for instance, the order of the position of the planets. An understanding of history requires an ability to place events in the proper chronological—or time—order. You will discover that to write effectively, you must be able to put ideas into a clear sequential pattern.

Because sequential order is so important to reading comprehension, textbook authors will often help you follow a sequence by using signal words such as the following:

first	after	later	following
then	before	last	finally
next	when	preceding	during

In a chronological order, you may also find dates (1878, May 12) and times (11:45, noon, evening).

When you see these sequence signal words in your reading, be alert for a sequence pattern of organization. With a sequence pattern of organization, what is important to learn is the correct order of the sequence. For example, in a set of directions, you must learn the correct order of the steps. If the sequence is chronological, you must learn what event occurred first, second, and so on.

As you read material written in sequential order, get into the habit of drawing a box around any signal words the author provides. This will help you become more aware of the order of the sequence. Notice how drawing a box around signal words makes them stand out and helps you follow the sequence in the following example:

In some cities police have been taught to cope with stress by a process

called stress-inoculation training. The program has three phases. In the first phase , the police officers meet as a group and talk about situations that make them angry, being spat on or called a name, for example. In the next phase , the officers learn to repeat to themselves statements that reduce stress. Some self-statements might be "I'm in control" or "This will be over shortly." In the final phase of the training, the officers act out with each other situations that might provoke anger and try out their new skills. They then watch their performance on video and get suggestions from other members of the group.

Notice that in this example the author lets you know that there will be three stages. Each stage is made clear by a signal word and by the repetition of the word *phase*. The next step for the reader is to mark the main idea and key words in the description of each phase.

In some cities police have been taught to cope with stress by a process called <u>stress-inoculation training</u>. The program has <u>three phases</u>. In the first phase , the police officers <u>meet as a group</u> and <u>talk about situations</u> that make them angry, being spat on or called a name, for example. In the next phase , the officers learn to <u>repeat to themselves statements</u> that <u>reduce stress</u>. Some self-statements might be "I'm in control" or "This will be over shortly." In the final phase of the training, the officers <u>act out</u> with each other situations that might provoke anger and <u>try out</u> <u>their new skills</u>. They <u>then watch their performance</u> on video and <u>get</u> <u>suggestions</u> from other members of the group.

Remember that what is important to learn in a sequence pattern is the order of the sequence. In this example, what is important to learn, then, are the three phases in stress-inoculation training.

EXERCISE 1

In this exercise first read each set carefully. Draw a box around any signal words that help you to recognize the sequence of the details. Then underline the main idea and key words in the sentences. Finally, after each set list the details in the correct sequential order indicated by the direction after the set.

Set 1   When Joan first got a job at the health clinic, she had very few duties. She greeted patients when they came in, asked whom they wanted to see, and told the doctor that they were there. After a few months, she began to answer the telephone and take messages. When she had been there six months, Joan was asked to take medical histories of new patients. She enjoyed her job so much that she enrolled in a nursing program.

List Joan's duties in the order that they were assigned to her.

_____

_____

_____

_____

_____

_____

Set 2   The way industry designs products has been virtually revolutionized by computer-aided design. First the engineer uses a special electronic pen to draw a three-dimensional design on a tablet connected to a computer. Then the computer is used to change and improve the design. Finally, when the engineer is satisfied with the design, the computer is used to analyze the design for problems.

List in order the steps in the process of creating a computer-aided design.

_____

_____

_____

_____

_____

Set 3   People wishing to start small businesses may qualify for loans from the Small Business Administration [SBA]. The procedure for applying for a loan is as follows. First the applicants must state what type of businesses are planned. They must also describe their experience and management qualifications. Next they must provide up-to-date financial statements listing all personal assets and liabilities. Then the applicants must estimate the amount they can invest and how much they will need to borrow. In addition, they must submit detailed descriptions of what they expect to earn in the first year the businesses are in operation. Finally, they must provide a list of collateral, properties to be turned over to the SBA if they fail to repay the loans.

List in order the steps in applying for a loan from the SBA.

_____

_____

_____

_____

_____

_____

Set 4   If a mentally ill person refuses hospitalization, there is a set procedure that must be followed before he can be legally committed. First a petition for the patient's commitment must be filed with the court. However, before the petition can be filed, a physician must examine the patient and sign a certificate stating that in the opinion of the doctor the person is mentally ill and in need of hospitalization. After receiving the petition, the court notifies the patient and appoints two physicians to examine him. A date is set for a hearing. The date cannot be set until the two physicians report that the patient is mentally ill. A judicial hearing is then held. Only after the completion of the hearing can the court order hospitalization.

List in order the steps for the commitment of a mentally ill person who refuses hospitalization.

_____

_____

_____

_____

_____

_____

Set 5 In Thessaly, the death of a family member initiates a long and elaborate ceremony that will continue for the next five years. Immediately after death, the body of the deceased is washed, dressed in formal clothing, and laid out in the family home to be visited and mourned by friends and relatives before being buried. During the years that follow, the female relatives visit the grave each night to light candles, talk to the dead, and see that the grave is well tended. After five years the bones are exhumed and cleansed in water and wine. Finally the remains are deposited in a common vault with the bones of others in the village who have died.[1]

List in order the steps in the Thessaly mourning ceremony.

_____

_____

_____

_____

_____

_____

Listing Pattern of Organization

A **listing** pattern of organization is used when there are several important pieces of information. This pattern is sometimes called an enumeration pattern because the author enumerates (numbers or counts) the several pieces of information for you. Most often in your textbooks the author describes a general term or category and then lists specific items in the general category. Read the following example and see if you can determine the general term or category and the specific items listed for that category.

> The "nontraditional" student does not fit into the eighteen to twenty-one age group who go to college immediately after graduating from high school. Among these students are found displaced homemakers—full-time homemakers who wish to join the work force because of divorce, widowhood, or economic reasons. Single parents, often on public assistance, are also part of this group of students. Retirees who find time weighing heavy on their hands may choose to fill that time by returning to school. Many veterans find their service-related skills not appropriate for civilian life and seek practical job skills while workers who have lost their jobs to technology or to the depressed economy seek new job skills. Finally, older workers still employed may need to upgrade their skills to be promoted.

The category in this example is "nontraditional students," and the specific types in this category (displaced homemakers, single parents, retirees, veterans, unemployed workers, and older employed workers) are listed. There is no particular reason to list displaced homemakers first or older employed workers last. In other words, there is *no particular order* in the list. The meaning of the paragraph would have been the same if the types of nontraditional students were listed in some other order. What is important to learn are the examples of students who are nontraditional.

Note that in this example the main idea is that the nontraditional student does not fit into the eighteen to twenty-one age group who go to college immediately after graduating from high school. The primary details list specific students who are nontraditional. Also note that there are two signal words that indicate a list: *also* and *finally*. Words that might signal a list are the following:

first	second	further	furthermore
in addition	another	other	then
besides	also	additionally	
moreover	next	finally	

Often what is listed in your college textbook are technical terms and their definitions. Usually the terms in the list are not pointed out by signal words; instead, they may be printed in colored ink, boldface, or italics. Look at the following example:

William Sheldon, in conducting studies to see if personality traits were linked to body type, identified three basic body types. The **endomorph** has a round, soft overweight body. The **ectomorph** is fragile and skinny with sharp angles. The **mesomorph** is muscular, athletic, and physically strong.

Note that the signal word *three* alerts you to look for a list of three body types. What is important to learn from this paragraph are the definitions of the three body types.

Sometimes when technical terms are listed, there is no topic sentence. The main idea is implied. Study the following example:

A firm that does business in the state in which it is incorporated is defined as a **domestic corporation.** A firm that does business in states other than the state in which it is incorporated is defined as a **foreign corporation.** A firm that does business in a nation other than the one in which it is incorporated is defined as an **alien corporation.**

The main idea seems to be that there are three types of corporations. The three primary supporting details are the definitions of the three types of corporations. What is important to learn is the definitions of the three types of organizations.

When you recognize that a listing pattern is being used, you need to decide what is being listed and make sure that you mark each item in the list. What is important to learn are the items that are listed.

EXERCISE 2

The following paragraphs are typical of what might be found in a study skills text from a chapter discussing how to take tests. These paragraphs all have information organized in a listing pattern. Box any signal words. Under each paragraph describe what is important to learn. The first is done for you.

1.   One technique for taking any test is to preview the test before beginning

to answer the questions. The test taker should look over the test to see

how many questions there are and what sort of questions are being

asked. Planning one's time so that each part of the test is allotted a specific amount of time is another technique that should be employed. In addition, most successful test takers recommend that the easiest questions be answered first so that points will not be lost on those if time runs out. Another technique is to review all answers before the test is handed in. In general answers should not be changed unless the test taker can articulate [express clearly] the reason the new answer is better than the original answer.

What is important to learn: Four techniques for taking a test.

2. In general, objective tests require that the test taker recognize the correct answer rather than recall it. The three most common types of objective tests are multiple choice, true-false, and matching. The multiple choice test requires that the test taker recognize the correct answer usually from among three or four choices. The true-false test requires that the test taker recognize statements as correct (true) or incorrect (false). Finally the matching test requires that the test taker be able to recognize which of the items in one column is best paired with an item in another column.

What is important to learn: _____

3. A multiple choice question is usually made up of two parts. The *stem* appears first and is a partial sentence. The *options* are the choices listed under the stem. The test taker is to choose the option that best completes the stem.

What is important to learn: _____

4. One of the most common mistakes that test takers make when answering multiple choice questions is to choose the first choice that seems correct.

It is important to understand why this is a mistake. Typically among the options there will be one completely wrong answer called a *distractor*, then there will be two partially correct answers, and finally there will be one answer that is more nearly complete or correct than the others. If the test taker chooses the first answer that seems correct, it may be one of the partially correct answers rather than the one most nearly complete or correct. To avoid this common mistake the successful test taker always reads all the options before making a choice.

What is important to learn: _____

_____

5.   Unsuccessful test takers often mistakenly look for a pattern when choosing answers for multiple choice answers. Usually the test is not constructed so that the correct answers fall into any sort of pattern. Another mistake is not choosing an option they believed to be correct because the letter or number of that option has already been used a number of times. Unsuccessful test takers also fail to choose an option believed to be correct because it makes the question seem too easy. In addition, they choose a particular option not because it seems correct but because it is totally unfamiliar.

What is important to learn: _____

_____

Compare and Contrast Pattern of Organization

If an author wants to make clear how one thing is similar to another, she will **compare** them. If what is important is how the two things are different, the author will **contrast** them. Sometimes the author will tell how the things are alike (compare them) *and* tell how they are different (contrast them) as in the following example:

Both the expert student and the nonexpert student are motivated to study. Both set aside regular periods of time each day to study. What makes the difference is how effectively each uses that study time. The expert student has a specific goal when he sits down to study. The nonexpert will not have a goal or will have a goal so general that it is not useful. For example, the goal of a nonexpert student might be "study" or "study Chapter 8 for the test on Friday" whereas the expert student's goal will be more specific such as "from Chapter 8 be able to list the steps in compounding interest daily."

Note that the author begins by telling how the expert and the nonexpert student are alike: Both are motivated to study and both set aside regular daily study periods. Then she goes on to describe how they are different: The expert student is able to set specific goals to make study time effective. Did you notice that the similarities are signalled by the word *both* whereas the contrast between the two students is signalled by the word *difference?* What is important to learn in the example is how the expert student is like the nonexpert student (comparison) and how the expert student is different from the nonexpert student (contrast).

The chart below lists signal words that indicate a comparison and those that signal a contrast.

Comparison	Contrast
both	difference
similar	different
similarities	while
like	whereas
alike	although
same	on the other hand
in a similar manner	on the contrary
	however
	instead

Sometimes you will find that the advantages of something are being contrasted to the disadvantages. In other words, you will be told the good points and the bad points of something. What is important to learn, of course, is what are the advantages and what are the disadvantages.

The pattern of organization can help you determine what is important to learn. Look for signal words to help you decide if the pattern of organization is a comparison or a contrast. If a contrast is being made, what is important to learn is how the two things are different. If a comparison is being made, what is important to learn is how the two things are alike. If the two things are both compared and contrasted, then it is important to know both how they are alike and how they are different.

EXERCISE 3

In this exercise, the information is organized in a compare or a contrast pattern. As you read each paragraph, box any signal words and decide whether a comparison or contrast is being made. Then in the space beneath each paragraph, write what is being compared or contrasted. That is what is important to learn in a compare and contrast pattern. The first one is done for you.

1.   The court system in America is composed at the federal and state level of trial courts that hear a wide range of cases. The majority of criminal and civil cases are heard by these courts. In contrast, the appellate courts hear appeals from the general trial courts. Appeals are filed in cases where the party receiving the unfavorable judgment feels that the case was wrongly decided.

     What is important to learn: The difference between trial courts and appellate courts.

2.   The invention of the assembly-line manufacturing technique is attributed to Henry Ford, who used it to manufacture the Model T Ford. Each worker on the line has a specialized task and performs that task as the product moves past him on the conveyer belt. The advantage of the system is that the number of work hours required to complete a product is reduced, thus lowering the production cost of the product. The disadvantages of the system are for the most part concerned with the impact on the worker. Most workers find assembly-line work routine, competitive, and boring. They often grow inattentive, which leads to mistakes and accidents.

     What is important to learn: _____

3. This passage is taken from a sociology book, from a section discussing the 1956 research findings of Melvin L. Kohn on child-rearing practices among American parents.[2]

> Kohn found that working-class families tended to punish children on the basis of what a child did. That is, if a child was prohibited from jumping up and down on the couch or yelling and then did so, the child was punished. In contrast, middle-class parents tended to be more concerned about the motives behind the behavior than about rule violations as such. Thus, if a child broke a rule against yelling in the house, the parent would punish on the basis of why the child yelled. Yelling done out of anger or a loss of self-control would tend to be punished. But if it was done out of enthusiasm or happiness, middle-class parents would ignore it. In effect, working-class parents reinforce conformity to external authority, while middle-class parents reinforce self-control and self-expression.

What is important to learn: _____

_____

4.   Every society has a set of rules called **norms** that prescribe appropriate behavior. Norms are made of up of **mores** and **folkways.** Mores [pronounced "morays"] are rules that normal people in the society are expected to obey. An example of mores in American society is that while men may appear on a public beach with their upper bodies uncovered, on most beaches women are expected to keep their breasts covered. On the other hand, while still a rule of behavior, folkways are not as strongly enforced as mores. We expect people to refrain from spitting in public, for example, but a person who violates this folkway, while arousing disgust, will not be arrested. However, a person who violates mores is subject to strong disapproval and perhaps even arrest.

What is important to learn: _____

_____

5.   The reading process is similar to the writing process. Both are a form of communication using the written word. The job of the writer, however, is to convey his or her message in a clear manner. The job of the reader, on the other hand, is to extract from the written page as accurately as possible the information being communicated.

What is important to learn: _____

_____

Cause and Effect Pattern of Organization

You get into your car after class, ready to go home. You turn the key and nothing happens. What do you do? You probably start to search for the **cause** of the **effect** of your car not starting. A cause is a reason whereas an effect is the outcome, result, or consequent of the cause. One thing is important to remember about causes and effects. In reality, the effect cannot precede the cause. The cause must come first. However, in reading, the author may talk about the effect before discussing the cause. You can test yourself to make sure you have not confused the cause and the effect by asking "Which had to have happened first?" That will be the cause.

Much of the information in college texts consists of causes for effects. Because this is such an important concept, let's take some time to make sure you are able to identify causes and effects. Remember, the cause is the reason that the effect occurs. The cause comes first. However, the cause does not necessarily come first in a sentence that describes cause and effect. Note the following examples. In each case, the cause is the same (Jim's car will not start) and the effect is the same (Jim must take the bus). But notice how different the sentences are. Also notice the signal words in boldface print.

1.   **Since** his car will not start, Jim must take the bus.

2.   Jim must take the bus **since** his car will not start.

3.   **Because** his car will not start, Jim must take the bus.

4.   Jim must take the bus **because** his car will not start.

5.   Jim's car will not start; **consequently** he must take the bus.

6.   Jim's car will not start; **as a result,** he must take the bus.

7. Jim's car will not start; **therefore,** he must take the bus.

8. Jim's car will not start, **so** he must take the bus.

9. The **effect of** Jim's car not starting is that he must take the bus.

10. Jim must take the bus **as a result of** his car not starting.

EXERCISE 4

Study the preceding sentences. For each sentence write the signal word in the first column below and write whether the word signals a cause or an effect in the second column. The first one is done for you.

Signal Word   **What the Word Signals**

1. since _____   cause _____

2. _____   _____

3. _____   _____

4. _____   _____

5. _____   _____

6. _____   _____

7. _____   _____

8. _____   _____

9. _____   _____

10. _____   _____

EXERCISE 5

Box any signal words you find in the following sentences. Then beneath the sentence write the cause and the effect.

1. I did not study for the test and consequently expect to fail it.

   Cause: _____   Effect: _____

2. Because I expect to fail the test, I did not study for it.

   Cause: _____   Effect: _____

3. I did not study for the test and, as a result, failed it.

   Cause: _____   Effect: _____

4. Since I expect to fail the test, I did not study for it.

   Cause: _____   Effect: _____

5. I expect to fail the test since I did not study for it.

   Cause: _____   Effect: _____

6. I did not study for it, so I expect to fail the test.

   Cause: _____   Effect: _____

7. I expect to fail the test as a result of not studying for it.

   Cause: _____   Effect: _____

8. I did not study for the test and therefore failed it.

   Cause: _____   Effect: _____

9. I did not study for the test; the outcome was that I failed it.

   Cause: _____   Effect: _____

10. The effect of not studying was that I failed the test.

    Cause: _____   Effect: _____

Now let's look at an example of a paragraph that is organized using a cause and effect pattern. This paragraph is typical of one that might be found in a psychology book in a section discussing alcoholism. The cause and effect signal words have been marked for you.

Withdrawal of alcohol from the chronic alcoholic may [result] in an acute psychosis known as **delirium tremens.** It is thought that faulty carbohydrate and protein metabolism, suboxidation of the brain, and malfunctioning of the liver [cause] metabolic disturbances in the patient.

The patient may see or hear things that aren't there [because] of hallucinations. [Since] the mind is clouded, the patient may be confused about where he is. Muscular tension may [cause] the fingers to extend.

A good way to organize material such as this is to make a chart so you can sort out the causes from the effects using the signal words to help. Let's use that approach on this paragraph.

Signal Word	Cause	Signal Word	Effect
	withdrawal of alcohol	result in	delirium tremens
	faulty metabolism, suboxidation of brain, malfunction of liver	cause	metabolic disturbances
because	hallucination		see or hear things not there
since	mind clouded		confused
	muscular tension	cause	fingers extend

The cause and effect pattern is a most important one for textbook comprehension. You must be able to separate cause and effect and not get them confused. Try using a chart like the one above to help you get them straight.

EXERCISE 6

For each of the paragraphs below find the causes and effects and list them beneath the paragraphs. Be alert for signal words; box them when you find them, and use them to help you identify the causes and the effects. The first one is partially done for you.

1. This passage is typical of what might be found in a text on study skills from a section on test taking.

   On test day if you find your mind going blank, your palms sweating, and you have an overwhelming desire to flee the room, you are experiencing test anxiety. The anxiety is caused by fear, and the fear is caused by a lack of confidence that you know the material. The most effective solution is to remove the fear by practicing answering questions you have predicted will be on the test. Having confidence in your knowledge of the material will result in a significant reduction in test anxiety.

Cause	Effect
fear	anxiety
lack of confidence	_____
_____	reduction in test anxiety

2. This paragraph is typical of one that might be found in a history book, in a section discussing the industrial growth of America in the later nineteenth century.

   One reason that the United States experienced such a strong economic growth during this period was the richness of the soil, which resulted in large harvests. In addition, labor was plentiful because of the flow of immigrants. Since there were no threatening neighbors, the citizens did not need to be concerned with supporting a large army so that money instead could be devoted to trade.

Cause	Effect
_____	_____
_____	_____
_____	_____
_____	_____
_____	_____

3. This paragraph is typical of what might be found in an introductory computer science textbook, in a section discussing the impact of computers on national elections.

> Are there problems when television networks make election predictions based on computer analysis of early returns from key precincts? Politicians firmly believe there are. Because the polls close three hours later on the West Coast than in the East, the networks are predicting who has won even before many people on the West Coast have voted. Some people believe the result of these early predictions is that West Coast voters decide not to vote, believing their vote will not count. Others say that West Coast voters are influenced by early predictions into voting for the declared winner.

Cause   **Effect**

_____   _____

_____   _____

_____   _____

4. The following passage from an astronomy book is taken from a section discussing the moon and its effect on the earth. The series of periods (. . .) indicates that material from the original has been left out.[3]

> Gravitational forces in the earth-moon-sun system cause **tides,** or bulges in the shape of the earth and the moon. The closer two objects are, the stronger the gravitational force each exerts on the other. Thus, the side of the moon facing the earth has a stronger force on it than the far side because the facing side is closer. . . . As a result, the moon stretches slightly along this line, limited by the small elasticity of its rock interior.

Cause   **Effect**

_____   _____

_____   _____

_____   _____

5. The following passage is taken from a geology book, from a section discussing earthquakes entitled "Damage."[4]

In urban areas, another major cause of property damage due to earthquakes is the fires started by crossed electric wires and broken gas lines. These fires cannot be controlled because of broken water mains and disrupted communications. In general, private homes have not been too badly damaged in most recent earthquakes. This is because the usual wood-frame house is a reasonably flexible structure. In some cases, the home may be too badly damaged to be salvageable, but it rarely collapses, killing the occupants. Particularly in many older homes the damage may be in the form of the building being pushed off its foundation. Most modern building codes require a tight bond between the foundation and the building. Typically the part of the average home which is damaged in an earthquake is the chimney. Because it is made of brittle bricks, a chimney tends to be cracked or fall down.

Cause	Effect
_____	_____
_____	_____
_____	_____
_____	_____
_____	_____
_____	_____

Four Patterns of Organization

Let's pause a minute to sum up what has been said so far in this chapter. The pattern of organization is the way the author has chosen to arrange the information being communicated to the reader. The importance of being able to recognize patterns of organization is that the pattern can help the reader determine what is important to learn.

There are four common patterns of information in college textbooks. A **sequence** pattern arranges the information in a *particular order* and what is important to learn is the order of the sequence. A **listing** pattern enumerates the information in *no particular order*. What is important for the reader is to identify what sort of list is given, for example, a list of terms and definitions or a list of items in a category. The reader should be sure to learn all the items in the list. In a **compare and contrast** pattern the similarities and/or differences of two things are given. The reader must learn whether similarities are being given (comparison) or whether differences are given (contrast). In some cases the author will tell both how the two things are alike as well as how they are different. In still other cases advantages (good points) are contrasted to disadvantages (bad points). A **cause and effect** pattern gives reasons (causes) for results (effects). What is important is that the reader identify the causes and the effects correctly.

In the following exercise there are examples of each type of pattern of organization.

EXERCISE 7

For each of the paragraphs below, box any words that signal a pattern of organization and in the space provided name the pattern of organization used. Decide what is important to learn from each paragraph, using the pattern of organization to help you.

1. This passage is typical of one that might be found in a business text, from a section discussing the management of small businesses.

   For the small business owner, the advantage of maintaining a large inventory [stock available for sale] is that sales are not lost because the desired product is not available and return business is more likely. The disadvantage is that a large inventory means that money must be spent for warehousing, taxes, insurance.

   Pattern of organization: _____

   What is important to learn: _____

2. This passage is typical of what might be found in a textbook for business management or accounting courses; it is from a section discussing how employees might be compensated (paid).

How much a new employee is paid depends on several factors. One factor is how much the company can afford to pay. Another is how much the competition is paying its employees for the same type of job. Often the cost of living in the area must be taken into consideration, especially for upper-level managers. Finally, government legislation such as the minimum wage scale must be considered.

Pattern of organization: _____

What is important to learn: _____

3. The following passage is taken from a book on reading and study skills, from a chapter that discusses how memory is stored in the brain.[5]

There are two kinds of memory: short-term memory and long-term memory. Short-term memory merely involves reading or listening to a fact or idea and immediately understanding it. All learning begins with short-term memory. The information in your short-term memory may be forgotten almost immediately if you do not actively work to remember it. Forgetting, you must realize, is a much easier process than remembering. Facts or ideas that do stay with you are stored in what is known as the long-term memory. You must work at keeping information in your long-term memory.

Pattern of organization: _____

What is important to learn: _____

4. The following passage from a psychology textbook is from a section entitled "Hearing Impairment."[6]

In conduction deafness, air waves are not able to reach the mechanism of the inner ear. This situation can be the result of a variety of causes, some as simple as a buildup of wax in the external ear. Other causes for conduction deafness include the hardening of the tympanic membrane and the destruction of the tiny bones within the ear which eventually stimulate the basilar membrane in the cochlea. Diseases that can create middle-ear pressure can also damage portions of the hearing mechanism.

Pattern of organization: _____

What is important to learn: _____

5. The following passage is typical of one that might be found in a study skills textbook in a section discussing study methods.

A proven method for effective textbook reading is the SQ3R method developed by Francis Robinson. The first step is to survey (the *S* step) the chapter by reading the title, introduction, section headings, summary, and by studying any graphs, tables, illustrations or charts. The purpose of this step is to get an overview of the chapter so that you will know before you read what it will be about. In the second step (the *Q* step), for each section you ask yourself questions such as "What do I already know about this topic?" and "What do I want to know?" In this step you also take the section heading and turn it into a question. This step gives you a purpose for reading the section. The third step (the first of the 3 *R*'s) is to read to find the answer to your questions. Then at the end of each section, before going on to the next section, you recite (the second of the 3 *R*'s) the answers to the questions that you formed in the question step. When you recite you should say the information you want to learn out loud in your own words. The fifth step is done after you have completed steps 2, 3, and 4 for each section. You review (the last of the 3 *R*'s) the entire chapter. The review is done much as the survey was in the first step. As you review, hold a mental conversation with yourself as you recite the information you selected as important to learn. The mental conversation could take the form of asking and answering the questions formed from the headings or reading the summary, which lists the main ideas in the chapter, and trying to fill in the details for each main idea.

Pattern of organization: _____

What is important to learn: _____

Mixed Patterns of Organization

Sometimes in your textbooks the author will organize the information using more than one pattern of organization. For example, often a listing pattern and another pattern of organization will be used. There may be a list of similarities, in which case you will have a listing pattern and a comparison pattern. Or perhaps a list of causes or a list of effects will be given. In general, if you identify a listing pattern, you will need to go one step further to see what is being listed. You will need to know whether you have a list of causes, effects, similarities, differences, or whether the list you have identified is, in fact, in a particular order, a sequence. What is important to learn is not just that there is a list but rather what is being listed.

Study the paragraph below in which there are two patterns of organization, a cause and effect pattern and a contrast pattern. The boxes indicate the words that signal a pattern of organization.

Since the expert student sets specific goals for his study time he will know when he has studied enough. He has studied enough when he can accomplish the goal he has set for himself. The nonexpert student, on the other hand, will not know that he has studied enough because his goal is stated in such general terms that he does not know what must be done in order to accomplish it.

Now study the diagram of the paragraph below:

- Signal word: on the other hand
- Pattern signalled: contrast
- What is being contrasted: the difference between expert and nonexpert student

- Signal word: since
- Pattern signalled: cause and effect
- Cause: expert student sets specific goals
- Effect: expert student knows when he has studied enough

- Signal word: because

- Pattern signalled: cause and effect

- Cause: nonexpert student's goal stated in general terms

- Effect: does not know when he has studied enough

Notice that in this paragraph it is not enough to know that the expert and nonexpert student are different. What is important to learn are the *reasons* the two students get *different results*. Both the contrast pattern and the cause and effect pattern help you decide what is important to learn.

Remember that reading is a thinking process. The most important thing you can do as a thinking reader is to engage in a questioning process as you read. In the passage above you might hold a conversation with yourself something like the following:

- What is important to learn here?

- I see by the signal words *on the other hand* that the expert and the nonexpert student are being contrasted.

- Is it enough to know that they are different?

- I see by the signal words *since* and *because* that causes are being given for effects. Can I use that pattern to decide more about the contrast between the expert and the nonexpert student?

- Well, the results that the expert and the nonexpert student get are different. So, that is what makes the expert student different from the nonexpert student: the results or effects he gets. Now, what causes can I find for the different results?

- What is important to learn are the causes for the different results that the expert and the nonexpert student get.

Let's try one more example. The following passage was taken from a book designed to help people improve their thinking and learning skills.[7] It is taken from a section entitled "Communication across Cultures," which discusses the difficulty we encounter when we try to communicate with people of different cultures. The boxes indicate words that signal a pattern of organization, and the underlined words indicate key phrases in the primary details and the main idea.

Many attempts to communicate involve nonverbal as well as verbal messages. Like verbal messages, nonverbal messages can also be misinterpreted across cultures. For instance, patterns of eye contact can have different implications for communication. In America, it is generally considered <u>important</u> to "<u>look people in the eye</u>." If, when meeting an American, you glance at his or her eyes and then quickly look elsewhere, you will frequently be perceived as unsure of yourself or perhaps rude. In <u>other</u> cultures, <u>however</u>, direct eye contact can <u>have other meanings</u>. For example, <u>in some American Indian tribes young children</u> are <u>taught</u> that it is <u>disrespectful to look</u> an <u>elder in the eye</u>. <u>Non-Indians who value</u> <u>eye contact</u> can <u>therefore</u> seem disrespectful to Indians. <u>Analogously</u>, <u>American Indian children</u> are often <u>perceived by white teachers</u> as <u>dis-</u><u>interested</u> <u>because</u> the <u>children look away</u> from the teachers rather than <u>look them in the eye</u>.

The signal words *like, different, other, however,* and *analogously* signal a compare and contrast pattern. What is being contrasted? We are being told that nonverbal messages such as eye contact patterns have different meanings in different cultures. Is that all that is important to learn?

The signal words *therefore* and *because* point out a cause and effect pattern. Are the causes or effects being contrasted? The cause is the difference in the meanings of eye contact patterns and the effect is that people from different cultures misunderstand the meanings.

Put the two patterns together and what is important to learn is that the **difference** in the meanings of nonverbal messages in different cultures can **cause** the **effect** of people from different cultures misunderstanding each other.

EXERCISE 8

The following selections have more than one pattern of organization. For each selection below, mark any pattern of organization signal words, determine the patterns of organization and write them in the space provided. Then use the patterns to help you decide what is important to learn and write it in the space provided. The first is done for you.

1. The following paragraph is taken from a sociology book from a chapter entitled "Organizations and Bureaucracy."[8]

   ### Types of Formal Organizations

   The sociologist Amitai Etzioni (1964) <u>distinguishes</u> among organiza-tions based on the <u>factors that lead</u> people to join them. <u>Some</u> orga-nizations are <u>voluntary</u>; individuals enjoy considerable freedom in determining whether to join or withdraw from them. Political parties, religious groups, hobby clubs, and fraternities and sororities are examples of voluntary organizations. Other organizations are coercive; people are compelled to enter them. Examples include prisons, concentration camps, custodial mental hospitals, and military institutions based on a draft. Still other organizations are utilitarian; people join them for practical reasons. Business and work organizations are illustrations of utilitarian organizations.

Patterns of organization: <u>Contrast, cause and effect, listing</u>

What is important to learn: <u>Different reasons people join organizations</u>

2. The following is taken from a psychology textbook from a section entitled "The Psychology of Facing Death."[9]

Death anxiety has several causes. First, there is the fear that the moment of death may be painful. Second, there is the fear of losing everything we enjoy in this life. Even people with a strong faith in life after death are subject to that fear. No matter how sure you are that you will live again, you will certainly not be living as you did in this life, with its particular set of pleasures.

Third, the fact that one's life will eventually come to an end casts doubt on the meaningfulness of life. Consider: The day will come when you die. A hundred years later, everyone you ever knew will also be dead. When there is no one alive who remembers you, will it make any difference how you lived your life?

But, you may say, I expect to become a famous person. My memory will survive. Perhaps. But how many people are remembered two or three hundred years after their deaths?

Moreover, the day will come when the entire human race will become extinct. Even if we avoid nuclear war and other immediate threats, the universe will, according to physicists, eventually either collapse into a black hole or else continue to spread out and cool until it is just one vast, lifeless expanse. Either way, the universe will then contain no life and no evidence that life ever existed. When that comes, will it make any difference how you lived or even whether you lived?

Death is one of the central philosophical problems of life. To live well, we must somehow cope with our death anxiety and preserve some sense of meaning, purpose, and value.

Patterns of organization: _____

What is important to learn: _____

3. This selection was taken from a business text from a chapter on promotional strategy.[10]

Samples are free gifts of a product. They are an attempt to gain public acceptance of the product that will result in future sales. Samples are particularly useful in promoting new products. Coupons are advertising inserts or package inclusions that are redeemable by the customer. Offering what amounts to a small price discount, they can be helpful in getting consumers to try a new or different product. Premiums are small gifts to the consumer for buying a product. They, too, are helpful in introducing a new product or getting consumers to try a different brand. Trading stamps are similar to premiums in that they are redeemable for additional merchandise. Historically they have been used to build loyalty to a certain retailer or supplier.

Patterns of organization: _____

What is important to learn: _____

4. This selection was taken from a psychology book from a chapter entitled "Origins: The Beginnings of Life."[11]

Three Stages of Prenatal Development

Each of the three stages of prenatal development has its own characteristics. Let's look at what happens in each stage.

During the **germinal stage** (fertilization to two weeks), the zygote enters a period of rapid cell division resulting in an increasingly complex organism that possesses rudimentary body organs, and such protective and nurturing organs as the *umbilical cord*, which connects the embryo to the **placenta,** the organ that brings oxygen and nourishment to the baby and absorbs its body wastes, and the **amniotic sac,** the membrane that encases the fetus.

In the **embryonic stage** (two to eight weeks), the embryo grows quickly and its major body systems (respiratory, alimentary, and nervous) and organs develop. Because of this rapid growth and development, this is the most vulnerable time for prenatal environmental influence. Almost all developmental birth defects (such as cleft palate, incomplete limbs, and blindness) occur during the critical first **trimester** (three-month period) of pregnancy. This is the time when growth is most rapid and the organism most vulnerable. Three out of four **spontaneous abortions** (miscarriages) also occur during this time, affecting an estimated 30 to 50 percent of all pregnancies. Chromosomal abnormalities are found in half of all spontaneous abortions. (Ash, Vennart, & Carter, 1977).

The **fetal stage** (eight weeks to birth) begins with the appearance of the first bone cells and is characterized by rapid growth and changes in body form.

Patterns of organization: _____

What is important to learn: _____

5. This selection was taken from a sociology book from a chapter entitled "Social Inequality."[12]

For our purposes we shall define **prejudice** as an irrationally based negative, or occasionally positive attitude toward certain groups and their members.

What is the cause of prejudice? Although pursuing that question is beyond the scope of this book, we can list some of the uses to which prejudice is put and the social functions it serves. First, prejudice simply because it is shared, helps draw together those who hold it. It promotes a feeling of "we-ness," of being part of an in-group—and it helps define such group boundaries. Especially in a complex world, belonging to an in-group and consequently feeling "special" or "superior" can be an important social identity.

Second, when two or more groups are competing against one another for access to scarce resources (jobs, for example), it makes it easier if one can write off his or her competitors as somehow "less than human" or inherently unworthy. Nations at war consistently characterize each other negatively, using terms that seem to deprive the enemy of any humanity whatsoever.

Third, psychologists suggest that prejudice allows us to "project" onto others those parts of ourselves that we do not like and therefore try to avoid facing. For example, most of us feel stupid at one time or another. How comforting it is to know that we belong to a group that is inherently more intelligent than another group! But how good it is that we do not belong to that group—the one everybody knows is lazy!

Of course, prejudice also has many negative consequences, or *dysfunctions*, to use the sociological term. For one thing, it limits our vision of the world around us, reducing social complexities and richness to a sterile and empty caricature. But aside from this effect on us as individuals, prejudice also has negative consequences for the whole of society. Most notably, it is the necessary ingredient of discrimination, a problem found in many societies—including our own.

Patterns of organization: _____

What is important to learn: _____

Summary

The way that the information in a textbook is arranged is called the pattern of organization; it is determined by what is important about the information that the author wishes to convey. There are four common patterns of organization used in college texts: sequence, listing, compare and contrast, and cause and effect. Often signal words will point out the pattern of organization. For example, if the pattern is cause and effect, signal words such as *result, consequently, because,* and *since* may alert the reader to look for causes (reasons) for effects (results).

If the reader recognizes that a particular pattern of organization has been used, he or she can use the pattern to decide what is important to learn about the information. If there is a compare and contrast pattern, for instance, the reader knows to look for similarities and/or differences. If there is a sequence pattern, what is important to learn is the order of the sequence.

Mixed patterns of organization are very common in college textbooks. If the reader recognizes that there is a listing pattern, very often there will be another pattern to help the reader decide what is being listed. There may be a list of causes for effects (cause and effect pattern), a list of advantages and disadvantages (compare and contrast pattern), or events in a time order (sequence pattern).

8　Reading for Studying

In the preceding chapters of this book you have learned those skills essential for reading college texts. You learned how to figure out unfamiliar words by using context clues and word parts. You discovered how understanding sentence structure helps in understanding the essential thought of a sentence and how understanding the structure of a paragraph helps in recognizing the main idea and primary supporting details of the paragraph. You learned how to use the pattern of organization to decide what is important to learn from a passage. In this chapter you put all those skills to work as you learn how to read to study.

There is a difference between reading and studying. Reading is the process of receiving a written message, and you have learned that the message has not been communicated if the reader does not understand the message. On the other hand, studying is the process of storing the information so that it can be recalled later. You know from your own experience that reading and studying must be different. Have you ever read a chapter in a textbook and then were not able to recall the information on a test? So you know that just reading the information does not guarantee that you will be able to recall it later.

Often when students are asked if they have studied for a test, they will reply, "Yes, I read the chapter three times." Now, rereading a chapter may enable you to remember more than if you only read it once. It is the repetition or repeated exposure to the material that helps you remember. But even if you have read a chapter three times, you still may have trouble remembering the information. In addition, if reading and studying are different processes, then rereading the material is still not studying it.

Reading for studying is more than just receiving the message conveyed in print, more than just getting the information. When you read to study, you intend that you will be able to recall the information later. Think for a moment about how you read the sports page of the newspaper. Usually you do not read the sports page in order to be able to recall the information later. You are reading primarily to get the information. Reading for studying includes getting the information and also reading in order to recall the information.

In this chapter we discuss three important aspects of reading for studying. First, you cannot remember what you do not understand. So one aspect of reading for studying is comprehension monitoring or checking your understanding. Second, you cannot learn everything in your textbook, so another aspect of reading for studying is deciding what is essential to learn. Finally, information gathered in reading must be organized in a way that makes it easier to learn. Therefore, organizing material to be learned is a third aspect of reading for studying.

Monitoring Comprehension

You cannot remember what you do not understand. Reading comprehension is the ability to understand a printed message. In the first chapter of this book we said that there were two things you could begin doing to increase your reading comprehension: improve your concentration and become an active reader by previewing a chapter before reading, asking questions as you read, and marking the textbook. In addition, all the skills you have learned as you worked your way through this book were skills to help you improve your reading comprehension. However, strange as it may seem, some students don't realize that they don't understand what they are reading because they do not know that they don't understand. Unfortunately, too many students don't know if they understand the material until they take a test; then they find out that they didn't know what they thought they knew. A better approach, of course, is to find out *before* the test if you know what you think you know.

How do you find out if you know what you think you know? The best way is to prove to yourself that you have understood the material you have been reading. You can do this by paraphrasing, putting into your own words, the important points the author has made. Some students recite or say aloud the important ideas; other students prefer to summarize the main ideas and important details either in outline or paragraph form. What is important is not how you prove to yourself that you have understood but that you *do* prove it by paraphrasing the important points and either reciting them or writing them out in summary form.

The process of proving to yourself that you understand the material is called **comprehension monitoring.** The word *monitor* means "to keep a check on." Comprehension monitoring is "stop and go reading." For example, one way to monitor your comprehension is to look at a section heading and before reading it, make a prediction about what you will learn in that section. When you have finished reading the section, stop and compare what you read to your prediction. Was your prediction accurate? What did you learn that was different from your prediction? If the material is unfamiliar, turn the heading into a question and read to find the answer to your question. When you find it, mark the key words and use the margin to write a paraphrase or summary of the answer. Marking your text in this way provides visual proof that you have been concentrating on the material and comprehending it. When you look back at the section, you will feel a sense of pride and accomplishment. Then stop at the end of the section and recite *in your own words* the answer to your question. If you cannot answer the question using your own words, you probably don't fully understand the information and need to reread the section.

Some students prefer to write out their answers on a piece of paper. They do this for each section and when they have finished, they have a summary sheet from which they can review the chapter. Do not go on to the next section until you can prove to yourself that you understand the section you have just read. Always check the accuracy of your answer by looking back at the text. If you have done a good job of marking, the answer will be easy to find. When the material you are reading is particularly hard, you might want to write in the margins in your own words the important points that were made in each paragraph. Doing this will ensure that you understand the material and will also increase your concentration as you read, because you know that when you finish reading the paragraph you are going to have to write out the important points.

This may seem like an awful lot of work. It is, because learning is a lot of work. That comes as a surprise to many students. Reading a chapter through passively is not as much work. But reading passively is also not learning. If you are interested in learning and knowing that you have learned, then you must be prepared to do more than simply read the chapter through in a passive or nonactive manner.

Deciding What Is Essential to Learn

A common complaint among first-year college students is that everything in their textbooks looks important and that they are uncertain about what is essential to learn. What is essential to learn depends on the course and the instructor. Making the decision about what to learn from the textbook is a decision you have to make in the context of the course you are taking. Here are some suggestions to aid in that decision.

First, examine the course syllabus. Most instructors give students a course syllabus, or outline, on the first day of class. This outline contains information such as the name of the instructor, office location, office hours, and the name of the text required for the course. The outline may also list topics to be covered in the course, sometimes by week, and the reading assignments, also sometimes by week. There may be a listing of course objectives or outcomes that explain what the student is expected to be able to do at the end of the course. Finally, there may be a list of dates for tests and projects.

Read the course outline carefully to see if it indicates in some way what you are expected to learn. Look for a list of topics to be covered in the course, and then look for a list of course objectives or expected course outcomes.

Now examine the chapter in your textbook. What parts of the chapter appear to be about a topic listed on the course outline? What parts of the chapter would help you achieve an objective listed on the course outline?

For example, the course outline for a psychology course might list "Describe three forms of group therapy" as a course objective and might list "Different forms of therapies" as a topic to be covered in the eighth week of the course. When you examine the chapter assigned for the eighth week, you note that there is a section of the chapter headed "Group Therapy." Now you know that this section is essential to learn.

A second way to decide what is essential to learn is to examine your classroom notes. Instructors do not spend class time going over material that is not important. Those topics discussed in class that are also in your textbook are very important. Look at your notes from class. What are the topics of the lectures for the week the textbook chapter is assigned? What parts of the chapter seem to discuss those topics?

A third way to make decisions about the essential material to learn is to listen for clues from the instructor. When the instructor assigned the chapter, did he or she emphasize that you read a certain part? For example, in a psychology class the instructor might say, "When you read Chapter Seven, be sure to look closely at the part on group therapy."

Often an instructor will make a remark such as this at the very end of the class, sometimes even as students are leaving. It is important, therefore, that you continue to listen closely at the end of the class and write in your classroom notes any remark the instructor might make about reading the assigned chapter. Don't count on simply remembering the remark when you sit down to do the reading.

Many students seem to believe that the last five minutes of a class are not important. They close their notebooks, put away their pens, pack up their books, stop listening, and start thinking about what they are going to do next.

Consequently, they often miss some of the most important things said in that class hour.

A final suggestion for deciding what is important to learn in a textbook chapter is to examine the chapter itself. Look at the beginning of the chapter for a list of important points to be made in the chapter. The introduction may outline the topics that will be discussed. Chapter objectives may be listed at the beginning of the chapter. In addition, look at the headings for each section. The heading is a title for that section, identifying the topic to be discussed. Look also for words in bold print, italics, or colored ink. These words are being emphasized as important. Look for notes in the margins. Sometimes margin notes are little summaries of the important material in a particular section.

Finally, look at the end of the chapter. The summary will list the important topics discussed in the chapter. There may be questions at the end of the chapter. The answers to these questions are the important points the author wants the reader to know.

Once you have identified the particular parts of the chapter that are essential to learn, the next question becomes "What in this section is essential?" Because main ideas are the points made about the topic, main ideas are certainly important to learn. Because the primary details support and explain the main ideas, they too are important to learn.

Organizing Material to Be Learned

After you determine what is essential to learn, that information must be organized. One method of organizing material to learn is to mark your text as you read it so that the important points stand out. Then extract the important points you have marked and organize them onto an outline or a chart.

Because you know that the main idea of a paragraph can be anywhere (not just the first sentence), you should read the paragraph through before marking anything. As you read, search for those sentences that express the main idea and primary details. Box any signal words you think point out the main idea or primary details. Then go back and decide which sentences express the main idea and primary details and mark the key words in those sentences. Marking key words rather than the entire sentence will help you concentrate more fully on what you are reading. It forces you to be an active reader because you must always be asking yourself "What should I mark in this sentence? What words express the essential thought of this sentence?" It will also help you keep a check on your comprehension. If you cannot decide on the key words to mark, it is probably because you do not understand the sentence. If you go through several pages of the textbook without marking anything, you have not been concentrating.

As you read the section also look for the pattern of organization because that will help you decide what is important to learn from the section. Box any signal words you find and note the pattern in the margin. For example, if you decide that the pattern is cause and effect, write "c/e" in the margin. Then when you find a cause, write "cause" in the margin, and when you find an effect, write "effect" in the margin.

Now let's see if we can put all this to work. Let's say that you are taking a psychology course and that you have decided that it is essential to learn about group therapy. You find in your text a section entitled "Group Therapy." Read the following passage and notice how it has been marked.

Group Therapy

[1] Although it is the appropriate treatment for some persons, individual therapy has certain disadvantages. In the *listing* first place, a number of sessions over a relatively long period of time may be needed before progress is evident, *disadvantage* and individual sessions are expensive. In addition, some clients may be unresponsive because they fear or mistrust *disadvantage* authority figures and cast the therapist in that role. Finally, if the client is experiencing social maladjustments, individual therapy does not provide an opportunity *disadvantage* for the therapist to observe the client engage in social interactions with a group of people. We will look at three of the most familiar types of group therapy.

[2]   The first type of group therapy is the **problem-centered** *listing* group. The purpose of this type of group therapy is to help group members with a specific, identified problem. *purpose* lem. Alcoholics Anonymous is an example of a problem-centered group. The therapist initially assumes a leader- *role of therapist* ship role and encourages the group members to respond freely to him and to each other. Group members are

encouraged to be <u>supportive</u> of each other and to <u>interpret</u> the <u>words</u> and <u>actions</u> of each other thereby serving as a reality checking mechanism. If the client is not being honest, the group members will quickly tell him so. Thus in a problem-centered group, the <u>client has both</u> the <u>emotional support</u> of the group members <u>and</u> a <u>constant challenge</u> to be honest with himself and with the other members. The <u>client</u> also experiences the <u>sharing</u> of <u>coping strate-gies</u> by group members, is <u>encouraged</u> to <u>adapt</u> those <u>strategies</u> to his own situation, and is <u>asked</u> to <u>report</u> on his <u>progress</u> at each group session.

role of group member

[3]   Another type of group therapy is the **training group** or "T-group." The <u>aim</u> of this type of group therapy is to <u>improve</u> the <u>understanding</u> of <u>group dynamics</u>. These groups are sometimes called "encounter groups" or "sensitivity groups." Unlike the <u>problem-centered group</u>, the T-group therapist at first <u>assumes</u> a <u>nonresponding role</u> so that the group appears leaderless. As the group members struggle together to achieve certain tasks, <u>they reveal</u> to the therapist, to the other members, and to themselves their <u>customary pattern of behavior</u> in group situations.

listing

purpose

contrast
role of therapist

[4]   A third type of group therapy is **family therapy** in which the <u>therapist meets regularly</u> with the members of the <u>nuclear family</u> (father, mother, children), <u>significant relatives</u>, or members of the <u>extended family</u> (grandparents). <u>Activities</u> in this type of therapy might <u>include</u> *psychodrama* in which family <u>members switch roles</u> and <u>act out</u> a <u>situation</u> that has caused trouble at home. For example, the son might take the role of the father and the father

listing

activities

the role of the son and act out a situation where the father (played by the son) disciplines the son (played by the father). A family member thus has the opportunity to see himself as others in the family see him. The therapist's role is to observe the interpersonal relationships and through questions and interpretations of behavior help the family members establish a rational and effective system of communication.

role of group member

role of therapist

Here is a list of the main ideas in the selection:

- Paragraph 1: Individual therapy has disadvantages.
- Paragraph 2: One type of group therapy is the problem-centered group.
- Paragraph 3: The training group is another type of group therapy.
- Paragraph 4: Family therapy is a third type of group therapy.

The next step is to decide on the pattern of organization. This will help you determine what is important to learn. Notice that there is a listing pattern signalled by "the first type," "another type," and "a third type." Remember that when a listing pattern has been identified, there is almost always another pattern that is more helpful in deciding what is important to learn. Because there are three types of group therapy, there must be something different about each type. Notice in paragraph 3 the contrast signal word "**unlike** the problem-centered group." What is important to learn seems to be how the three types of group therapy are different.

Using the main idea of each paragraph and the contrast pattern of organization, ask yourself "What else do I need to know about this?" The answer to that question will help you decide what primary details are essential to learn.

- Paragraph 1: What else do I need to know about the disadvantages of individual therapy? Further question: What are the disadvantages?

- Paragraph 2: What else do I need to know about problem-centered groups? Further question: How are problem-centered groups different from other types of group therapy?

- Paragraph 3: What else do I need to know about T-groups? Further question: How are T-groups different from other types of group therapy?

• Paragraph 4: What else do I need to know about family therapy? Further question: How is family therapy different from other types of group therapy?

Complete the outline in Exercise 1 using these questions as a guide to selecting essential information and looking at the primary details that have been marked. The outline is partially filled in to help you.

EXERCISE 1

   I. Individual therapy has three disadvantages

      A. _____

      B. Clients who mistrust or fear authority figures may be unresponsive

      C. Therapist cannot _____

   II. One type of group therapy is the problem-centered group

      A. The purpose is to _____

      B. The therapist assumes leadership role and encourages members to respond freely

      C. Group members _____

      D. The client has emotional support and is challenged to be honest

      E. The client also _____

  III. The training group is another type of group therapy

      A. The purpose is to _____

      B. The therapist _____

      C. Group members _____

  IV. Family therapy is a third type of group therapy

      A. The therapist meets with _____

      B. Activities _____

      C. Family members _____

      D. Therapist's role _____

EXERCISE 2

Using the outline you completed in Exercise 1, answer the questions below as true (T) or false (F). Do not look back at the selection. If you have done a good job of deciding what is essential to learn, you should be able to answer these questions using just your outline.

_____ **1.** One disadvantage of individual therapy is its expense.

_____ **2.** In individual therapy, the therapist cannot observe the client in social interactions.

_____ **3.** If the client mistrusts authority figures, individual therapy is best for him.

_____ **4.** In problem-centered groups, the client hears how others cope with the same problem he has.

_____ **5.** The purpose of the T-group is to help members deal with a particular, identified problem.

_____ **6.** In the training group, the therapist performs the same function as in the problem-centered group.

_____ **7.** The therapist assumes a leadership role in the T-group.

_____ **8.** In family therapy, the therapist meets with members of the nuclear family.

_____ **9.** Psychodrama is a technique in which group members share coping strategies.

_____ **10.** The role of the family therapist is to help family members learn to communicate effectively with each other.

EXERCISE 3

Read the following paragraphs. Underline key words in the topic sentences. Box signal words that point out a pattern of organization. Use a questioning process to determine essential primary details. Then for each paragraph, fill in the outline with the main idea and essential primary details. For the first two selections a skeleton outline is provided. You are on your own for the last one.

1. There are two compelling arguments to support the abolition of capital punishment. First, it does not deter crime. Studies have shown that the crime rate has not declined significantly in those states that have capital punishment. In addition, there is always the possibility that an innocent person will be put to death. For example, there are many known cases of mistaken identity that resulted in an innocent person being convicted of a crime.

Main idea   I. _____

Primary detail   A. _____

Primary detail   B. _____

2. The most obvious reason to take lecture notes is to have them for review. For example, material given in lecture often cannot be found else-where—in the textbook, for instance. However, taking lecture notes can also help the student concentrate on the lecture. It is difficult to day-dream while taking notes. In addition, since material given in lecture that also appears in the text is most likely to be on a test, it is important to take notes so students can compare lecture material with the text to locate any repetition of information. One of the most valuable skills students can possess is the ability to take lecture notes in an organized, efficient manner.

Main idea   I. _____

Primary detail   A. _____

Primary detail   B. _____

Primary detail   C. _____

3. Despite statistics that indicate an increase in the number of missing children, many authorities do not believe that the problem has grown significantly greater in the last ten years. These authorities explain that

the number of *reported* cases has increased but that the *actual* number of cases has remained steady. Experts also claim that some children are falsely reported missing when the parent knows exactly where they are. Falsely reporting a child missing has become a legal tactic employed to gain custody rights. The reporting parent is well aware that the child is with the divorced partner and claims the child is missing in an effort to influence the court. Additionally, the public has been made more aware of the problem. The practice of putting pictures of missing children on milk cartons has brought the problem to the breakfast table. Public awareness has also been increased by television movies.

Main idea   _____

Primary details   _____

                             _____

                             _____

                             _____

EXERCISE 4

In a psychology class you have been told to be prepared to discuss why some children have difficulty learning to read. In your textbook you find the following section entitled "Reading Disabilities."[1] Read the section and determine the pattern of organization. Then mark main ideas and primary details in each paragraph. Finally, arrange the essential material on a chart.

Some children (and some adults) never learn to read well, even though they have normal intelligence. This condition is known as **dyslexia.** The two major types of dyslexia (Boder, 1973) are described below.

In the more common type of dyslexia, children cannot read words by sounding them out. They may look at the word CAT, sound it out "Kuh, Ah, Tuh," and still not recognize that the combination spells *cat.*

With practice, such children learn to read a moderate number of words by the whole-word method, but they continue to be baffled by new or unfamiliar words. When they come to a new word, they tend to guess at it from the context, ignoring the letters. If they are unfamiliar with the word *city*, they may read it as "Los Angeles." Although children with this kind of dyslexia have trouble learning to read English, they easily learn to read Chinese characters, saying the English equivalents (Rozin, Poritsky, & Sotsky, 1971). In Chinese, each character represents a word, not a unit of sound.

In the less common type of dyslexia, children can sound out the words but cannot recognize a word as a whole. They read very slowly, sounding out every word, even the most common ones, as if they were meeting each word for the first time. They have particular trouble with words that have irregular spellings (which are common in English) such as *laughter, knife,* or *phlegm.* Their spelling is accurate only when a word is spelled the same way it sounds. Typical errors include "lisn" (for listen), "sed" (for said), and "bisnis" (for business).

A good reader recognizes any common word as a whole and can sound out any unfamiliar word when necessary. You do not have to sound out each word you encounter letter by letter. Occasionally, however, when you come across an unfamiliar word like *hemianopsia* (meaning blind in half of the eye), you may have to stop and sound it out and divide it into parts.

Some adult readers, however, continue to move their lips as they read, even though it slows down their reading (McCusker, Hillinger, & Bias, 1981). Many deaf people, incidentally, move their *hands* as they read, converting the written word into sign language just as hearing people convert it into speech. (Treiman & Hirsh-Pasek, 1983).

EXERCISE 5

The following passage is longer than any you have examined so far in this book. Don't be overwhelmed by its length. Take it one paragraph at a time. Box signal words that point out main ideas and details. Be on the alert for words that signal the pattern of organization. Remember that there may be more than one pattern of organization. Use the pattern of organization to help you decide what is important to learn. Then use the main ideas and primary details to find the essential material. Finally, make an outline of the material that you have decided would be essential to learn.

This passage is taken from a section in an economics book discussing who should pay for higher education, in a chapter entitled "Economics of Higher Education."[2] The series of periods (. . .) that you will see in this selection is called an ellipsis and is used to show that some of the original text from the economics book has been left out. Four periods (. . . .) are seen when the omission follows a complete sentence; in that case the first period is the final punctuation of the preceding sentence.

Sometimes the production or the consumption of a product yields benefits to people who neither produce nor consume it. Suppose my wealthy neighbor hires an orchestra to play at her garden party and I am not invited. She pays for the pleasure of her guests. But who is to stop me, a lover of beautiful music, from listening to its haunting strains from my side of the property line? The production of the music yields *social spillover benefits.*

. . . The widespread provision of educational services is generally thought to have social spillover benefits. It is believed by many that over and above the direct benefits to the individuals who receive them . . . there are additional benefits to the society as a whole. Some of the spillovers commonly cited are reduced fire hazards, reduced crime rates, improved community sanitation techniques and facilities, better government services to the community, more enlightened citizens who make the society a more pleasant place in which to live, and a better functioning democratic process stemming from greater voter literacy.

. . . If social benefits from higher educational services exist, the use of state taxing powers and state support of higher education sufficient to pay for those benefits would seem to be reasonable. . . .

. . . The other major argument for state support of higher education is that it enables capable but poor students to obtain a college or university education. Education serves to increase the capacities of human resources to produce and to earn income. Since poor families do not have the means of paying for higher education for their children, and this is not the fault of the children, the state can do much to enable them to escape from poverty by providing them with the same kind of educational opportunities that are available to the children of middle- and higher-income families.

The case has much merit. One of the generally recognized functions of governments in the modern world is that of mitigating poverty. In the United States, very substantial parts of both state and federal budgets are for this purpose. . . . It seems reasonable that state support of higher education for the poor should be an integral and important part of any antipoverty program.

. . . There are two main arguments why students should pay for their own education. These are that (1) those who benefit are the ones who should pay, and (2) economic resources would be used more efficiently, that is, some waste would be avoided.

The argument that those who benefit should pay is an equity argument. It asks why one group of persons—taxpayers—should be forced to pay a part of the educational costs of another group—students and their families. To be sure there will be some overlapping of the two groups; students and their families are also taxpayers. However, a much larger proportion of taxpayers are not college and university students, and neither are their children. Many of these are poor families. . . . Is it equitable for the state to levy taxes that rest partly on poorer nonstudent families to help pay for the education of children from middle-income and wealthy families?

. . . Another argument for student self-support is that people tend to waste whatever is free to them and to economize or conserve whatever they have to pay for. . . . If higher educational services are provided at reduced or free tuition costs to students, the incentive to economize on or make the best possible use of the resources providing those services is weakened—so the argument runs. Low tuition induces students who have no interest in learning to attend the university whereas higher tuition charges would make them or their parents think more carefully about whether or not they should do so. Further, those who do attend would be inclined to make more of their opportunities if they cost more. There would be less inclination to waste professors' time or to destroy property.

Summary

Reading is the process of receiving information in written form and is therefore an act of communication. Reading comprehension is improved by removing distractions to concentration and by participating actively in the reading process. Studying is the process of storing information so that it can be recalled later. Reading for studying involves using comprehension monitoring as a check on understanding, deciding what is essential to learn, and organizing material to be learned.

Comprehension monitoring is the act of keeping a check on one's understanding. Recitation after each section of answers to self-made questions and important points made in the section is one way of proving that one has understood the message of the section. Marking the text as one reads facilitates (makes easier) comprehension monitoring.

Decisions about what is essential to learn from a textbook chapter must be made by you in the context of the course. The course outline (syllabus) should be examined for lists of important topics. Classroom notes should be examined for mention of topics that also appear in the textbook. Remarks by the instructor concerning the reading assignment may help you decide what is essential to learn. The textbook chapter itself should also be examined. Introductions, chapter objectives, headings, words in different type, margin notes, summaries, and questions at the end of the chapter are all helpful in determining the important points in the chapter.

In order to organize material to be learned, you must first find the main idea and primary details of each paragraph in a section of the chapter that you have decided is essential to learn. Asking "What else do I need to know?" about each main idea can help you select the essential primary details. The pattern of organization of the information can also help you decide what information is essential to learn. The information can then be organized in an outline or arranged on a chart.

Notes

Chapter 2

1. Louis E. Boone and David Kurtz, *Contemporary Business* (New York: The Dryden Press, 1985), pp. 6, 10, 40, 63, 68, 281, 438.
2. Diane E. Papalia and Sally W. Olds, *Psychology* (New York: McGraw-Hill, 1985), pp. 316–17, 323, 378, 528.
3. Papalia and Olds, pp. 73–74.
4. Boone and Kurtz, p. 34.
5. Ansel M. Sharp and Richard H. Leftwich, *Economics of Social Issues*, 7th ed. (Plano, Tex.: Business Publications, 1986), pp. 68, 143, 330.
6. Edward J. Coburn, *Learning about Microcomputers: Hardware and Software* (Albany, N.Y.: Delmar, 1986), p. 14.
7. Helena Curtis and N. Sue Barnes, *Invitation to Biology*, 4th ed. (New York: Worth, 1985), pp. 15–16.

Chapter 4

1. S. Morris Engel, *The Study of Philosophy: An Introduction* (New York: Holt, Rinehart & Winston, 1981), p. 13.

Chapter 5

1. Patricia A. Potter and Anne G. Perry, *Fundamentals of Nursing: Concepts, Process, and Practice* (St. Louis, Mo.: C. V. Mosby Co., 1985), p. 730.

2. Kermit D. Larson and William Pyle, *Fundamental Accounting Principles*, 11th ed. (Homewood, Ill.: Richard D. Irwin, 1987), p. 59.

3. W. Edgar Moore, Hugh McCann, and Janet McCann, *Creative and Critical Thinking*, 2nd ed. (Boston: Houghton Mifflin, 1985), p. 132.

Chapter 6

1. Joseph F. Trimmer and James M. McCrimmon, *Writing with a Purpose*, 9th ed. (Boston: Houghton Mifflin, 1988), p. 157.

2. Diane E. Papalia and Sally W. Olds, *Psychology* (New York: McGraw-Hill, 1985), p. 197.

3. Ed Reynolds and Marcia Mixdorf, *Confidence in Writing: A Basic Text* (New York: Harcourt Brace Jovanovich, 1987), p. 49.

4. Lester A. Lefton and Laura Valvatne, *Mastering Psychology* (Boston: Allyn & Bacon, 1983), p. 171.

5. Anthony C. Winkler and Jo Ray McCuen, *Writing the Research Paper: A Handbook*, 2nd ed. (New York: Harcourt Brace Jovanovich, 1985), p. 34.

6. William T. Keeton, *Biological Science*, 3rd ed. (New York: Norton, 1980), p. 7.

7. *You and the Law*, Advisory ed. Henry V. Poor (Pleasantville, N.Y.: The Reader's Digest Association, 1971), p. 11.

8. James W. Kalat, *Introduction to Psychology* (Belmont, Cal.: Wadsworth, 1985), p. 411.

9. Trimmer and McCrimmon, p. 158.

10. Lea Masiello, *Writing in Action: A Collaborative Rhetoric for College Writers* (New York: Macmillan, 1986), p. 17.

11. Rodney Stark, *Sociology*, 2nd ed. (Belmont, Cal.: Wadsworth, 1987), p. 341.

12. Louis E. Boone and David L. Kurtz, *Contemporary Business*, 4th ed. (New York: The Dryden Press, 1985), p. 376.

13. *Understanding Psychology*, 3rd ed., rev. by James Hassett (New York: Random House, 1980), pp. 427–28.

14. R. Wayne Moody, et al., *Management Concepts and Practices*, 3rd ed. (Boston: Allyn & Bacon, 1986), pp. 167–68.

15. Henry L. Tischler, Phillip Whitten, and David E. K. Hunter, *Introduction to Sociology*, 2nd ed. (New York: Holt, Rinehart & Winston, 1986), p. 95.

16. E. Jerome McCarthy and William D. Perreault, Jr., *Basic Marketing: A Managerial Approach* (Homewood, Ill.: Richard D. Irwin, 1987), p. 164.

17. Kalat, p. 163.

18. Kalat, p. 272.

19. Lefton and Valvatne, pp. 264–65.

Chapter 7

1. Alexander Tsiarsas, "Mourning in Thessaly," *Science 83*, June 1983, pp. 66–67.
2. Rodney Stark, *Sociology*, 2nd ed. (Belmont, Cal.: Wadsworth, 1987), p. 154.
3. William K. Hartman, *Astronomy: The Cosmic Journey* (Belmont, Cal.: Wadsworth, 1987), pp. 84–85.
4. Robert J. Foster, *Physical Geology*, 3rd ed. (Columbus, Ohio: Charles E. Merrill, 1979), p. 252.
5. Peter E. Sotiriou, *Integrating College Study Skills: Reasoning in Reading, Listening, and Writing* (Belmont, Cal.: Wadsworth, 1984), p. 273.
6. Lester A. Lefton and Laura Valvatne, *Mastering Psychology* (Boston: Allyn & Bacon, 1983), p. 227.
7. John D. Bransford and Barry S. Stein, *The Ideal Problem Solver* (New York: W. H. Freeman, 1984), p. 111.
8. Donald Light, Jr., and Suzanne Keller, *Sociology* (New York: Alfred A. Knopf, 1985), p. 188.
9. James W. Kalat, *Introduction to Psychology* (Belmont, Cal.: Wadsworth, 1985), p. 411.
10. Louis E. Boone and David L. Kurtz, *Contemporary Business*, 4th ed. (New York: The Dryden Press, 1985), p. 334.
11. Diane E. Papalia and Sally W. Olds, *Psychology* (New York: McGraw-Hill, 1985), p. 392.
12. Henry L. Tischler, Phillip Whitten, and David E. K. Hunter, *Introduction to Sociology*, 2nd ed. (New York: Holt, Rinehart & Winston, 1986), p. 302.

Chapter 8

1. James W. Kalat, *Introduction to Psychology* (Belmont, Cal.: Wadsworth, 1985), p. 252.
2. Ansel M. Sharp and Richard H. Leftwich, *Economics of Social Issues*, 7th ed. (Plano, Tex.: Business Publications, 1986), pp. 68, 84–86.

Acknowledgments

Pp. 18, 115, 166: From Diane E. Papalia and Sally Wendkos Olds, *Psychology*. Reprinted by permission of McGraw-Hill Book Company.

Pp. 22–23, 183: From Ansel M. Sharp and Richard H. Leftwich, *Economics of Social Issues*, 7th Edition. Reprinted by permission of Richard D. Irwin, Inc.

P. 33: From Helena Curtis and N. Sue Barnes, *Invitation to Biology*, 4th Edition. Reprinted by permission of Worth Publishers, Inc.

P. 75: From S. Morris Engel, *The Study of Philosophy: An Introduction*, 2nd Edition. Reprinted by permission of the author.

Pp. 113–14, 123–24: From Joseph F. Trimmer and James M. McCrimmon, *Writing with a Purpose*, 9th Edition. Copyright © 1988 by Houghton Mifflin Company, pp. 157, 158. Used with permission of the publisher.

Pp. 116, 136, 160: From Lester A. Lefton and Laura Valvatne, *Mastering Psychology*. Copyright © 1983 by Allyn & Bacon, Inc. Reprinted by permission of the publisher.

Pp. 123, 132, 136, 165, 181: From James W. Kalat, *Introduction to Psychology*, © 1986 by Wadsworth, Inc. Used by permission.

Pp. 125, 151: From Rodney Stark, *Sociology*, 2nd Edition, © 1987 by Wadsworth, Inc. Used by permission.

Pp. 128, 167: Excerpts from pp. 95, 302 from *Introduction to Sociology*, 2nd Edition, by Henry L. Tischler et al., Copyright © 1986 by Holt, Rinehart & Winston, Inc. Reprinted by permission of the publisher.

Index